THE LUSITANIA'S LAST VOYAGE

THE LUSITANIA'S LAST VOYAGE

Being a Narrative
of the Torpedoing and Sinking
of the R. M. S. Lusitania
by a German Submarine
off the Irish Coast
May 7, 1915

BY

CHARLES E. LAURIAT, Jr.

ONE OF THE SURVIVORS

With Illustrations

Skyhorse Publishing

First published 1915

First Skyhorse Publishing edition 2016

Skyhorse Publishing books may be purchased in bulk at special discounts for sales promotion, corporate gifts, fund-raising, or educational purposes. Special editions can also be created to specifications. For details, contact the Special Sales Department, Skyhorse Publishing, 307 West 36th Street, 11th Floor, New York, NY 10018 or info@skyhorsepublishing.com.

Visit our website at www.skyhorsepublishing.com.

10 9 8 7 6 5 4 3 2 1

Library of Congress Cataloging-in-Publication Data is available on file.

Cover design by Matt Fetter
Cover image: Wikimedia Commons

Print ISBN: 978-1-5107-0867-9
Ebook ISBN: 978-1-5107-0879-2

Printed in the United States of America

TO MY FATHER

WHO TAUGHT ME IN BOYHOOD TO SWIM, AND
TO KNOW NO FEAR OF THE SEA

AND

TO MY MOTHER

WHO FOUNDED THE FAITH THAT
HAS BROUGHT ME
THROUGH ALL THINGS

I DEDICATE THIS
BOOK

CONTENTS

FOREWORD

Twenty minutes. Glance at a clock now and then; check it again when you finish this foreword. The time it takes to read these words may be all the time the crew and passengers aboard Cunard's *Lusitania* had to make life-or-death decisions on the afternoon of May 7, 1915. Imagine the shock of a torpedo blast on a sunny afternoon and the immediate, sickening list to starboard, while most passengers dozed in their cabins, finished lunch, played cards, or ambled around the deck, anticipating their imminent arrival in Liverpool. How would you have reacted? What would you have done?

Most books on the *Lusitania* disaster follow a

familiar formula. The reader is given background on the First World War, the role of neutral America, the British blockade of Germany, and the German decision to delineate a "War Zone" in the waters around Great Britain and declare unrestricted submarine warfare against any ships—neutral or belligerent, armed or unarmed—entering that War Zone. Readers are then introduced to passengers and crew, and shown the horrors of the German attack on a beautiful spring day, just off the coast of Ireland.

Charles E. Lauriat's incomparable eyewitness account of the atrocity is like none you've ever read before, and surely none you'll ever read. In the first place, it is short, in which not a word is wasted. Lauriat begins his account on the day of the attack. He has finished lunch and is strolling on the deck. He feels a jolt (the first torpedo), then another (the detonation of the American-made shells and cartridges stored in the ship's hold), and, in a flash, the lives of the 1,959 passengers and crew aboard are "on the clock."

THE LUSITANIA'S LAST VOYAGE

Tick-tock. The torpedo strike began the inexorable process by which great ships sink. One might hope that the "Lucy's" modern construction—its hull space divided into twelve watertight compartments—might save the liner, but one could not count on it. If portholes were negligently left open (they were) or the sliding doors between compartments opened to shovel coal (they were), then it was game over. Lauriat, an American bookseller headed to England on business, showed remarkable cool-headedness. His spare, lively account guides us around the ship as it foundered.

Lauriat had been leaning on the rail talking to a couple when the explosions rocked the ship. He immediately advised them to return to their cabin to get their lifebelts. Like many he encountered, they stood stock still, shocked into inaction. Lauriat descended to his cabin, put on his lifebelt, took his passport, cash and checks, grabbed an armload of lifebelts from a bin and returned to the main deck.

The *Lusitania* had more than enough lifeboats for the personnel aboard. But prompt decision-making was needed at every level. The captain had to order the lifeboats lowered; the crew had to fill them with "women and children first," then put the men aboard the last boats and lower them all into the sea.

Tick-tock. Pierced on its starboard side and rent internally by the explosion of the munitions stored in the bow, the *Lusitania* listed drastically, as water rushed in and filled the underwater compartments, thrusting the ship to the left and leaning it to the right. The ship's captain would later be cleared of wrongdoing by a court of inquiry, but Lauriat knew better. He was standing on the port side, assisting the crew in lowering lifeboats when Captain William Turner appeared and ordered them to stop. Turner insisted that the *Lusitania*, a state-of-the-art "greyhound" of the Cunard fleet, wouldn't sink—"she's all right," Turner said. A brave woman passenger already seated in a lifeboat doubted him in a polite voice: "Where do you get your information, Captain." "From the engine room, Madam," he barked back in less polite tones.

This was a critical error. There were eleven lifeboats on each side of the ship. Each boat could carry sixty passengers or more. But with the ship rolling hard to the right, it was essential to launch the portside lifeboats immediately. To wait even a minute more would mean that they would ascend high into the sky and swing inboard on their davits like Christmas ornaments.

Tick-tock. Events were happening so fast that Lauriat never had time to argue with the skipper over his decision to empty the portside lifeboats. Lauriat slid over to the starboard side and observed scenes of pitiful mayhem. Cunard's skilled crews had all been conscripted into naval service, so the crewmen trying to launch the lifeboats were second-stringers and rookies.

Tick-tock. Lauriat describes the terror of the passengers as they looked up now and saw the ship's four great funnels directly over them, as the ship lay nearly on its side. Nobody could cut the lifeboats loose; there were no axes to cut the ropes. Lauriat saw a man sawing at them with a pocketknife. No one could keep his feet any longer, as the ship was dunking bow first underwater and settling sideways into the deep. Lauriat saw one lifeboat, crammed with wailing women and children, still attached to the davits, plunge underwater with the ship's bow.

Tick-tock. Now there were just seconds to spare. Passengers who hadn't made it into a boat climbed like alpinists to the stern, which had begun to lift high in the air. It was a natural survival instinct, but one certain to end in death.

Tick-tock. Lauriat jumped and began to swim away as fast as he could. Big ships like the *Lusitania* create suction when they sink, dragging down everything in their vortex. Floating in the water, not far from the ship, he watched the "Lucy" slip beneath the waves. The day was clear, the water calm. He saw the passengers gripping the rails and watching the sea rush up to take them. He heard their last cries as they vanished.

The story continues and is not to be missed. Lauriat traveled on to London to complete his business. He presents the German press campaign to justify the sinking as well as the whitewashed Board of Trade investigation that cleared Captain Turner of any errors in his handling of the crisis. No summary such as this can do justice to the intimacy and immediacy of Lauriat's account. One must read it to know the full horror of those twenty minutes.

—Geoffrey Wawro
June 2016

THE ZONE

Avert Thy gaze, O God, close tight Thine eyes!
Glance down no longer on the ocean foam,
Lest Thou behold such horrors as can turn
Men's burning hearts to ice, and chill their souls.

Keep Thine heart warm and full of charity
That Thou mayst yet be able to forgive,
And pity feel for those who know not when
To pause in deeds of ruthless sacrifice.

Restrain Thy wrath, and keep Thine hand in
check;
Smite not, nor fiercely thrust without the pale
Those who can dare to strew the ocean waste
With fellow creatures, innocent of wrong.

Forget the studied purpose to destroy;
The launching of the missile through the deep;
The shattered hull; the crushed and bleeding forms;
The seething swirl of wreckage, women, men.

Remember that they know not what they do
Who strike in deadly fear and ghastly hate;
Remember that somehow, and at some time,
Each crime exacts its human penalty.

Remember that man's conscience and man's mind
Are agents of Thy purpose and Thy plan,
Which work within a deadlier revenge
Than any shrapnel shot or sabre thrust.

Remember that new generations come
Upon whom fall the burden and the curse,
The anguish of old hatreds and past wrongs,
The crushing debt, the struggle and despair.

Restrain, O God, the sweep of this vast hate;
Recall the nations to their sense of shame:
To those in blinding war, to us at peace,
Reveal anew the message of the Christ.

WILLIAM LLOYD GARRISON, JR.

(Reprinted by permission of the
author and of the Boston *Transcript*)

THE LUSITANIA'S LAST VOYAGE

PART I

THE LUSITANIA'S LAST VOYAGE

PART I

6, New Oxford Street, London, W. C.,
May 12, 1915

Our voyage from New York had been uneventful and in fact it was quite a "Lauriat Crossing"; fine weather, smooth sea, and after the first few hours of Sunday (May 2) there had been no fog up to Friday morning (May 7), when it came in for a short time.

The speed of the boat had not been what I had expected it would be, for after the first full run of 24 hours, in which we covered 501 miles, the run dropped each day to well below the 500 mark, and the last 24 hours up to

Friday noon (May 7) we made only 462 miles. This was partly accounted for by the fact that we picked up Greenwich time at Cape Clear and put the clock ahead 1 hour and 40 minutes.

The reason this small run impressed itself upon my mind was that I expected that when we sighted the Irish Coast the "Lucy" would show a burst of "top speed" and that we should go flying up at not less than 25 miles an hour. The run up to Thursday noon (May 6) had been 484 miles, and so confident was I that she would put on steam that I bought the high number in the pool (for Friday), which was 499. It was the only pool I went into and I couldn't help it, for the number sold at £3.0.0 and at that price it looked like a "bargain."

During the forenoon of Thursday (May 6) we swung out and uncovered 22 lifeboats, 11 on each side, showing Captain Turner's preparedness towards emergency. I was keenly interested in all that was done aboard ship as we approached the Irish Coast, and in fact all through the voyage I kept my eyes unusually wide open.

At night the shades in the saloon were closely drawn, and I noticed that my bedroom steward left a note for the night watchman stating just which ports were open when he (the steward) went off duty.

Friday noon when the run was posted I was surprised, for I certainly thought that this was the time to put on speed. The sea was smooth as a pancake, an ideal chance for a dash up the coast. When I heard the fog horn early Friday morning I turned over and took another snooze, for there was no use in getting up if it was foggy and disagreeable weather. The fog did not last long and was nothing more than a morning mist.

I got up at noon and had time for a stroll

around the deck before lunch at 1 o'clock. I noticed that we were not going anywhere near top speed and were following, as I remembered, the usual course up the Irish Coast, that being about 5 to 7 miles distant. I wondered at our loafing along at this gentle pace.

When I bought my ticket at the Cunard Office in Boston I asked if we were to be convoyed through the war zone, and the reply made was, "Oh yes! every precaution will be taken."

When we got into Queenstown I found the people furious through the act itself and disgusted that three torpedo-boat destroyers should have lain at anchor in Queenstown harbor all the time the Lusitania was coming up the Irish Coast. Some of the men along the sea front told me that these boats had been out during the morning, but had come back for "lunch." They all turned up after the tragedy, but they could have been used to better advantage before it.

After lunch I went to my stateroom and put on my sweater under the coat of the knickerbocker suit that I was wearing and went up on deck for a *real walk.* I came up the main companion-way and stepped out on the port side of the steamer and saw Mr. and Mrs. Elbert Hubbard standing by the rail, a little for'ard of the entrance. I joined them and was conversing with them when the torpedo struck the ship. In fact, Mr. Hubbard had just jokingly remarked that he didn't believe he would be a welcome traveller to Germany, owing to the little essay he had written entitled "Who Lifted the Lid Off Hell." Mr. Hubbard had not more than finished this remark when the shock came. This "essay" appeared in the "Philistine" for October, 1914, and Mr. Hubbard had given me a copy earlier on the voyage. If you want to read a piece of vitriolic English, I suggest that you send for a copy.

Where I stood on deck the shock of the impact was not severe; it was a heavy, rather muffled sound, but the good ship trembled for a moment under the force of the blow; a second explosion quickly followed, but I do not think it was a second torpedo, for the sound was quite different; it was more likely a boiler in the engine room.

As I turned to look in the direction of the explosion I saw a shower of coal and steam and some débris hurled into the air between the second and third funnels, and then heard the fall of gratings and other wreckage that had been blown up by the explosion.

Remember that I was standing well for'ard on the port side, and consequently looked back at the scene of the explosion, at an angle across to the starboard side; therefore, although the débris showed between the second and third funnels, I think the blow was delivered practically in line with the fourth funnel.

I looked immediately at my watch and it was exactly 8 minutes past 9 (A.M.) Boston time, which means 8 minutes past 2 Greenwich time.

I turned to the Hubbards and suggested that they go to their stateroom to get their life jackets. Their cabin was on deck B, on the port side, at the foot of the main companion-way, and they had ample time to go there and get back to the deck; but Mr. Hubbard stayed by the rail affectionately holding his arm around his wife's waist and both seemed unable to act.

I went straight down to my stateroom, which, as you will remember, was the most for'ard one on deck B on the starboard side. The boat had taken a list to starboard, but it was not acute, and so I had no difficulty in making my way to and from my cabin. I tied on a life belt, took the others in the room and my small leather case containing my business papers, and went up on deck to the port side. I went back to the spot where I had left the Hubbards, but they had gone, and I never saw them again.

I found those who needed the life belts, put them on, tied them properly, and then went aft along the port side of the ship, for I was confident that all hands would naturally rush to the starboard side and so there would be more opportunity to help along the port side. I turned and walked for'ard toward the bridge, and Captain Turner and Captain Anderson were both calling in stentorian tones not to lower away the boats, ordering all passengers and sailors to get out of them, saying that there was no danger and that the ship would float. A woman passenger beside me called out to Captain Turner in a perfectly clear and calm voice, "Captain, what do you wish us to do?" "Stay right where you are, Madam, she's all right." Then the woman asked him, "Where do you get your information?"—and he replied in rather a severe and commanding voice, "From the engine room, Madam." She and I turned and walked quietly aft and tried to reassure the passengers we met.

As I looked around to see to whom I could be of the greatest help it seemed to me that about everyone who passed me wearing a life belt had it on incorrectly. In their hurry they put them on every way except the right way: one man had his arm through one armhole and his head through the other; others had them on around the waist and upside down; but very few had them on correctly. I stopped these people and spoke to them in a calm voice and persuaded them to let me help them on with the belts, for they certainly stood no show in the water rigged as they were. At first they thought I was trying to take their jackets from them, but on reassuring them they let me straighten them out.

I had been watching carefully the list of the steamer, and by now I was confident that she wouldn't float and that the end was coming fast. I remembered one or two personal things in my stateroom which I very much wanted, and I figured that I had time to go down and get them. If I didn't come through the final plunge, I wanted to feel I had them with me, and if I did get through, I was just as sure I wanted them, so there didn't seem anything to do but to get them, which I did.

There was a companion-way for'ard of the main staircase, about half-way between it and my stateroom, so I went along the port passage inside of deck A, down that companion-way, and along the starboard passage to my stateroom. It was not until I walked along this passage that I realized how acute was the list of the ship. My stateroom was an inside one without a porthole, and consequently could be lighted only by electricity. I pressed the switch, but the light had gone, so I put my hand on a box of matches; for each night when I retired I placed a box in a particular place, just in case I needed it. With the aid of these matches I found the little article for which I was looking, opened my travelling bag, and took out some papers which included my passport and other envelopes that could easily be slipped into my inside pocket.

I had kept my drafts on my person, for I figured that there was no use in giving them to the purser, except as a precaution against theft, and that was negligible. If what had happened was to happen, I knew there would be no time to reclaim them from the purser.

I made my way back along the passage, walking in the angle formed by the floor and the side walls of the staterooms rather than the floor, and went back up the for'ard companion-way, the same that I came down. Going along the passage (on deck B) I looked down some of the cross passages that lead to the staterooms, and at the bottom of the ones I passed I saw that the portholes were open and that the water could not have been more than a few feet from them. Here let me state that I consider it most extraordinary that the portholes on the lower decks should not have been *closed* and *sealed* as we steamed through the war zone. At luncheon the portholes in the dining-saloon on deck D were open, and so I doubt not that all the others on that deck were open.

I mean those in the staterooms. I cannot speak with certainty in regard to the port-holes on deck E. I believe that the first list the ship took brought her down to these open ports on the starboard side and that she sank much more quickly from filling through them.

On my return to the deck I felt that the steamer must make her final plunge any moment now, and as there was nothing more that could be done on the port side—for there was no discipline or order with which to do it—I passed through to the starboard side. Men were striving to lower the boats and were putting women and children into them, but it seemed to me that it only added horror to the whole situation to put people into a boat that you knew never would be cleared and which would go down with the steamer; better leave them on the deck to let them take their chance at a piece of wreckage.

True, there was no panic, in the sense that anyone crowded or pushed his way to the lifeboats, but there was infinite confusion, and there seemed no one to take command of any one boat.

As I came out on the starboard side, I saw, a little aft of the main entrance, a lifeboat well filled with people, principally women and children, that no one had attempted to clear from the davits. The steamer was rapidly sinking, and I realized that the boat must be cleared at once if the people were to be saved.

I climbed into the stern of the boat, which was floating flush with the rail of deck B, so far had the steamer settled, and helped clear the fall. We freed our end and swung the ropes clear, but we couldn't make anyone for'ard understand what to do or how to do it.

I remember looking for'ard and seeing

someone, I think it was a steward, bravely cutting away at the thick ropes with a pocket knife. How I wish he had had an axe! What would I have given for one real sailor man for'ard; we could have saved that boatload of people. I started to go for'ard, but it was impossible to climb through that boatload of people, mixed up as they were with oars, boat hooks, kegs of water, rope ladders, sails, and God knows what — everything that seemed to hinder progress to getting for'ard. The steamer was all the time rapidly settling, and to look at the tremendous smokestack hanging out over us only added to the terror of the people in the boat. I certainly did not blame them, for it was a harrowing sight, even to one as familiar with the ocean as I am. However, I should have gone for'ard and made the try, except that the stern end of the boat was raised by a small swell of the ocean and I was impressed by the nearness of the davit by getting a blow on the back which nearly knocked me overboard.

Then I admit that I saw the hopelessness of ever clearing the for'ard davit in time to get the boat away, so I stepped out and made a try for it by swimming. I spoke to several and urged them to come; but truly they were petrified, and only my training from boyhood up, in the water and under it, gave me the courage to jump. I swam about 100 feet away from the ship and then turned around to see if anyone was following to whom I could lend a hand, and found several who needed encouragement. Also I wanted to see when the final plunge of the steamer came, that I might be the more ready to fight against the vortex and tell the others. The Lusitania did not go down anything like head first: she had, rather, settled along her whole water line. This convinces me that practically all the ports must have been open, even those as far down as Deck E. The stern did not rise to anything like a perpendicular, nor did it rise so high that I could see a single one of the propellers or even the end of her rudder. Not one of her funnels fell.

The last I saw of the lifeboat out of which I jumped was that she was being pulled down, bow first, as the tackle had not been freed and the stern of the boat was rising high in the air. While the people were thrown out, they were not so violently thrown as those from some of the lifeboats that were dropped when half lowered into the water.

There was very little vortex; there was rather a shooting out from the ship instead of a sucking in, after she sank; this I am told was *partly* caused by the water rushing into her funnels and being blown out again by explosions made by the mixing of the cold water of the sea with the steam of the boilers. I saw an interesting statement in one of the papers, purporting to have come from Captain Turner, in which he stated that the small amount of suction was probably due to the fact that the bow of the boat was already resting on the bottom when the stern went down. This seems quite feasible, as she sank in about 60 fathoms (360 feet) of water and she was 755 feet long.

The sea was wonderfully smooth, and it seemed to me that if one could keep clear of the wreck and pick up a lifeboat, that it could be manned and that we could go back and get many survivors. I was able to work this out quite as I planned.

As I waited for the final plunge something caught me on the top of my head and slipped down to my shoulders, pressing me under the water; I couldn't imagine what it was, but on turning to see I found that it was one of the aërials of the wireless that stretched from topmast to topmast.

The present style of life belt, or rather jacket, is not the old-fashioned kind filled with hard cork, but a larger and more bulky affair filled with fibre, and when you have it on you look and feel like a padded football player, especially around the shoulders. When I shook this wire off my head, it caught me around the shoulders on the soft pad, and I couldn't shake it off. It took me down under the water and turned me upside down. I tell you I "kicked." I came up none the worse for my ducking, for it simply reminded me of one of my various trips down to see "Susy the Mermaid" when I was a youngster at Camp Asquam and the older boys used to duck us youngsters anywhere from five to fifteen times a day, according to the unpardonable sins we were supposed to have committed; and these weren't mere "duckings" either. They used to push us under, put their feet on our shoulders, and then give a good shove, so that we went down anywhere from six to sixteen feet under water. I hated the duckings at that time, but they proved mighty good training!

When I came up, after shaking the Marconi wire, the waves bearing the wreckage and people were upon me. After swimming around and helping those I could by pushing them pieces of wreckage to which to cling, I saw a short distance away a collapsible lifeboat floating right side up, swam to it, and climbed aboard. A seaman quickly followed, and a fine husky chap he proved to be. I heard my name called, and for the moment I didn't realize whether it was a call from Heaven or Hell, but when I turned in the direction of the voice I found the man to be G——, one of the three men with whom I had played cards each evening. I pulled him up on the boat, and we three got out our jackknives and went at a kind of can-opening operation, which was really the removing of the canvas cover of the boat.

They call that invention a "boat," but to start with, it is nothing but a "raft." Let me try to draw you a word picture and see if you will understand it.

Suppose you floated a real lifeboat in the water, and at the water line cut down the sides so that the bottom of the boat that was left floated flush with the water. Then deck over and make watertight this part of the boat that is left. This gives you a round bottomed, watertight raft, floating almost flush with the water.

Take a long piece of about 24-inch high (or wide) canvas that will reach all around the sides from one end back to the same end. Nail the lower edge of this canvas to the outside edge of the "raft." To enable you to raise these "collapsible" canvas sides and to keep them in place, make a stout rail that will be curved to the shape of the floor of the "raft" and nail the top edge of the canvas on to it.

This now "collapsible boat," with its folding canvas sides, is of course shallow, and about three or four of them can be nested on the deck of a steamer in the space occupied by a "real lifeboat." There is a canvas cover laced down over the top of these boats, the same as on regular boats.

Before you can do anything with a collapsible lifeboat you must make it a "real boat" by lifting up its canvas sides and lashing them in place so they can't collapse. Until this is done you have nothing but a "raft." It is almost impossible to lift the rail into place if there are people hanging on to it, as that would mean lifting the people as well. Also, you can't lift the sides, which automatically raise the cross seats, if there is anyone lying across the boat, and you can't get on the "raft" without getting on the seats. We tried to persuade the people who were hanging on to the rail to take off their hands and hang on to the life ropes — but that was impossible. Never have I heard a more distressing cry of despair than when I tried to tell one of them that that was what we were doing. In their condition I don't wonder they thought we were trying to push them off. So we had to take some aboard, those who were in the most panicky condition, and try to get up the sides with the "raft" half covered with people.

The seats of these boats are attached to an iron brace which is supposed to slide on a metal run in the middle of the boat. A wooden brace at either end is held in place by a pin when the sides are raised to their proper height, but, as the saying is, "There warn't no pin" and the wooden brace in my end of the boat was broken and the metal run for the iron braces of the seats was so rusted and corroded that it wasn't a "run;" so there we were, back to a raft again.

Not an oar in the boat, nor even a stick with which to reach wreckage so that we could block up the seats. We must get those seats braced up to give us the protection of the canvas sides, and they mustn't fall down either, because then the "boat" became a "raft," the people became a little more panicky, and the falling seats hurt and slightly injured the people sitting between them, for of course we had to seat those too exhausted to pull and haul on the floor between the seats. We had to have some oars too to make the boat navigable, so we fished round in the wreckage and were fortunate to get five oars (one broken, but that served me as a steering oar) and some blocks. Then with a long heave and a heave all together we raised the blasted seats as far as possible, but not to their proper height, and jammed the blocks under them. We were lucky to get blocks that act as supports to a *real* lifeboat, which, as you know, have notches cut on the long side. These blocks are like little steps, so that we were able to shove them under the seats to the limit.

About the fifth man aboard the boat was a chap named B——; he was a husky, no mistake. He weighed about 200 pounds and was all good material. This man G—— was another good one too; he deserved his name. By this time we must have had fifteen people in our now "*non*-collapsible boat." Let us thank God for the "non."

I went aft and took the steering oar and my two huskies, B—— and the sailor man, rowed the heavy sweeps, and G—— stayed for'ard to help the people in. We headed back into the wreckage and picked up those who seemed most urgently in need.

I won't enter into the detail of the condition of the poor souls we got, but two instances of nerve stand out so clearly in my mind that I must tell them. Both pertain to women, and never have I seen greater courage and patience shown by anyone.

I heard a call near my end of the boat and told the boys to back water, and I reached over and pulled in a woman who I thought at first glance was a negress; I never believed a white woman could be so black. I learned afterwards that she and her husband had got into a lifeboat, and while he was busy helping to clear it she got panic-stricken by the tremendous overhanging funnels and jumped back on to the steamer without her husband knowing it. She was aboard when the final plunge came, and the suction took her part way down one of the funnels, but the thankful explosion blew her forth, out into clear water, in among the wreckage, where she could hang on. The clothes were almost blown off the poor woman, and there wasn't a white spot on her except her teeth and the whites of her eyes. Marvellous to say she wasn't hurt and proved a great help in cheering us all by her bright talk.

For coolness I think this second case is even more remarkable. We had about as many in our boat as we ought to take when I heard a woman's voice say, in just as natural a tone of voice as you would ask for another slice of bread and butter, "Won't you take me next? you know I can't swim." When I looked over into the mass of wreckage from which this voice emanated all I could see was a woman's head, with a piece of wreckage under her chin and with her hair streaming out over other pieces of wreckage. She was so jammed in she couldn't even get her arms out, and with it all she had a half smile on her face and was placidly chewing gum. The last I saw of her when I helped her off the boat at Queenstown was that she was still chewing that piece of gum, and I shouldn't be surprised if she had it yet. Of course, we couldn't leave her, and as there was no possible way that I dared try to get her without going into the water for her, I told her that if she'd keep cool I'd come after her. To my surprise she said it was not at all necessary, just hand her an oar and she'd hang on. That is the last thing in the world I should ever have dared to do, for naturally I thought, in view of the fact that she could not swim, that as soon as I cleared away the wreckage with an oar she'd get rattled and sink. After what she had said I got my huskies to back through the wreckage till my oar would reach to her. Then I placed it as close to her face as I could and she wriggled around and got her two hands on the oar, held fast, and we pulled her through.

Then we rowed for the shore. G—— took the for'ard port oar, and somewhere in the shuffle we had picked up a couple of the stokers, and while they weren't very big men they were red-headed cockneys and they were trumps. Their conversation was something to remember; I shall never forget it. They two rowed the for'ard starboard oar, B—— rowed the after port oar, and the sailor man rowed the after starboard oar. Others helped push on the oars and so we had a good crew. I steered for a lighthouse on the coast, for I didn't know whether the Marconi operator had had time to send out an S. O. S., or if he had, whether or not it had been picked up. It was a good long row ashore and I knew we could not get there until after dark, and it was much better to land on a shore, however barren, near a lighthouse than to land on that part where there might not be an inhabitant for miles; also I saw the sail of a fisherman between us and the lighthouse, so I had two goals for which to steer.

The lighthouse for which we were steering was that on the Head of Old Kinsale. There were already two real lifeboats between us and the shore. We had stayed around and picked up everyone who seemed to be in the most helpless condition. Those we were forced to leave were as safe as if we had overcrowded them into our flimsy craft. The calmness of the sea was the only thing that enabled us to take on so many, with any degree of safety.

We must have rowed about a quarter of a mile toward shore, when off in the distance I saw one lone man floating around by himself. He seemed to prefer his own society to anyone's else by going off "on his own," but apparently he had changed his mind and got lonesome, for he sure did yell. He looked safe enough, as he had one of the big round white lifebuoys around his body, under his arms, and he was perfectly safe from sinking. I was pretty sure that according to the rules of the blessed "Board of Trade" we had all the people in our boat that our license would allow us to carry. Still I headed for the chap, for you couldn't go off and leave that one more soul floating around. It was lucky we went for him for he was in pretty bad shape, but recovered all right after we got him ashore. This chap turned out to be McM——, a fine Canadian fellow and a man of some experience in shipwreck, for he was on the Republic when she sank.

After rowing about two miles we came up to the fishing smack, and although they had already taken on two boatloads, they made room for us. Before anyone left our boat

I counted heads and found we had 32 aboard! It wasn't just the time to hunt souvenirs, but I took my steersman's oarlock with me; it will do for a paper weight.

Aboard the fisherman I witnessed one of the most affecting scenes of all. It seems that the husband of the temporary negress we picked up was aboard, and as we approached she recognized him and called to him; but he stood at the rail with a perfectly blank expression on his face and refused to recognize his own wife. Not until we were directly alongside and he could lean over and look the woman squarely in the face did he realize that his wife had been given back to him.

The old fishermen did everything in their power for us; they pulled up all the blankets from their bunks, they started the fire and made us tea while tea lasted, and after that boiled us water. The old ship was positively slippery with fish scales and the usual dirt of fishermen, but the deck of that boat, under our feet, felt as good as the front halls of our own homes.

The sight aboard that craft was a pitiful one, for while most of the first two boatloads of people that got aboard were dry, many of them had in their excitement removed much of their clothing before getting into the boat and consequently were, by this time, pretty thoroughly chilled. Those in my boat were in the saddest condition, for each one had been thoroughly soaked and some of them had been through terrible experiences. There is practically no cabin on one of these little fishermen, so all hands had to stay on deck, except a few that were able to help themselves down into the so-called cabin. The worst injured of course had to stay on deck. I gave my sweater to a chap who had on nothing but an undershirt and a pair of trousers, and I loaned my coat to a woman until we got into Queenstown. There were not nearly enough blankets aboard for each to have one. There were over 80 people on that small boat.

After being aboard about an hour we were picked up by the steamer Flying Fish which had come down from Queenstown. We were made comfortable on this good old packet. You will remember she is a side-wheeler and one of the tenders that came out to meet the ocean steamers before they were not too proud to stop at Queenstown.

The ocean was so calm that when we transferred our passengers to the Flying Fish we were able to lay the fisherman alongside the steamer and those who could stepped across. The two boats lay so close and steadily together that we carried our cripples across in our arms. The smoothness of the ocean must have been a special dispensation from Heaven.

We were torpedoed at 8 minutes past 2. I went overboard and my watch stopped at 9:30 Boston time, 2:30 Greenwich. I figure I was in the water three or four minutes before my watch stopped. I think the sweater which I had on under my coat and the life belt that I had tied on made it slower work for the water to get at my watch.

We must have been an hour and a half getting the boat into shape and picking up the people from the wreckage, and we must have been rowing two hours before we reached the fishing smack at 6:00.

By 7:00 we were on the Flying Fish, and tied up to the pier in Queenstown at 9:15, so you see we fared quite well. It was quite ludicrous to be held up by the patrol boat at the mouth of Queenstown Harbour and to be asked in formal tones, "What ship is that?" and to hear the captain reply,

"The ship Flying Fish, with survivors of the Lusitania." Word was immediately given us to go on.

This is where there came very near being a real fight. It happened this way—Two steamers had passed the Flying Fish on the way in and were tied up at the Cunard dock ahead of us, so we were told to land at the dock below. That was all very well, but the captain informed us that we couldn't go ashore until he had reported to the "inspector." I knew that the 100 odd people that we had on the Flying Fish didn't care about any "inspector" that ever grew in the town of Queenstown, but what they wanted and needed and ought to have was hot drink and food just as soon as they could get it. The captain, with true Irish stubbornness, went to do his duty ashore as "he seen it." We let the captain get around the corner out of sight and then G—— and

I started to put the gangplank over, but were told by some figure standing on the dock that we must wait for the captain's return. We gave this figure, whom we presume was a guard, three seconds to get out of the way or get knocked down by the gangplank. He moved, and we ran out the gangplank and handed our passengers ashore. Those who were able to navigate by themselves walked up the streets to the various hotels. Then we got down to our two cripples: one was a man in our collapsible lifeboat and one a woman we found on the fishing smack. Each had a broken leg. And right here let me tell you an instance of nerve displayed by this man B——, whose leg was broken. We had taken him into our boat before we got the seats braced up, for he was in pretty bad shape and we were afraid to leave him longer in the water. He was in the bottom of the boat, partially sitting on one of the seats, and when we endeavored to heave up on them, I spoke to him rather roughly and asked him if he couldn't get off. He looked up to me with half a smile and said, "I would, old chap; but did you know I have a broken leg and can't move very fast?" I was careful how I spoke after that!

I went ashore to see if I could find an ambulance or stretchers. A little way up the street in front of the Cunard office I found about 20 Naval Reserve men drawn up in squares of four; each squad was armed with a folding canvas stretcher. They were as fine a lot of men as I ever saw, and when I told them I had two cripples and needed two stretchers they didn't wait there for any commands from a *real* officer; they just asked me where were they, and I marched them down to the boat double quick.

It was low tide when we got into Queenstown and consequently the landing had to be made from the top of the paddle box. This necessitated all hands going up a very narrow companion-way, built on the side of the paddle box and so too narrow and too steep to permit the carrying of a stretcher. I went aboard and carried the two cripples ashore on my back. To get them ashore this way must have hurt them terribly, but never a groan from the woman nor from the man. The fact that injured people could show such nerve as this gave us fellows who were not injured the physical strength to do all that we did do.

One of the women in our boat went along with the girl with the broken leg to the hospital, and so I felt she'd be well taken care of. This chap B—— refused to let anyone accompany him to the Marine Hospital, having perfect confidence in the four Naval Reserve men who carried the stretcher, and certainly that confidence was justified.

The last chap we picked up in the boat, McM——, had a badly sprained ankle, and as I seemed about the right height he was using me as a human crutch.

When we went up the street in Queenstown it was filled with people willing to help and do anything in their power to relieve our sufferings. I have heard stories of Scottish hospitality, but I never saw anything more spontaneous or genuine or more freely given than the Irish hospitality of Queenstown.

McM—— and I were in pretty good shape and were well dried off, and while his ankle pained him a good deal and I was pretty much cut up around the forehead and nose by the aërial, we were able to navigate by ourselves.

We went directly to the Post Office and I sent my "Safe and Sound" cable to you people. Then McM—— and I went up the street, and the hospitality of Queenstown storekeepers, inspired by the idea of making a few extra sales had caused them to open their shops at that time of night, and we went in and bought a couple of sets of pajamas of the thickest wool that I ever put on. "Out-sizes" they were, but they proved none too "out." About the second time they are washed I expect they will fit the boy, but they felt mighty comfortable that night.

We had quite a time finding a place to rest our weary heads and warm our chilled bodies. I kept away from the two main hotels, because I knew they were filled with the people who arrived on the first two steamers. When we got near the centre of the town I asked a native to tell us of some small place where we could get rooms. He directed us to the little hostelry "Imperial Bar." It was a perfectly appropriate name.

The hospitality of the manageress was "Imperial" and the "Bar" was good.

At the door we found a Mr. and Mrs. K——. He was badly injured. He had been brought to the hotel by the reserves on a stretcher. He was not in bad enough shape to go to a hospital, but he couldn't walk. The K——'s got a double room and McM—— and I took the other spare room.

He turned in and I turned out. I went down into the town, for I knew I could be of help to some of the survivors. I got back at midnight and went to bed. I didn't have to lie awake and think about going to sleep, for I had been standing and moving around under a strain for some 10 hours, so I just passed off into a dead, dreamless sleep. My clothes were almost dry, and I wasn't suffering from a chill. We have always heard that Scottish hospitality is accompanied by a draught of the national beverage, and in justice to the old landlady I must say that she didn't omit to give me a draught of the Irish national beverage. She told me it was made by her old grandfather, and certainly he knows how to make Irish whiskey! I woke up McM—— and we repeated the dose on him. He didn't cry at being waked up in a good cause!

Saturday morning I was up and dressed at six o'clock, and the dear old woman gave me a dish of tea and some bread and butter in the kitchen, and I started for the town to buy some raiment for people that I knew were practically destitute. I had dressed in the kitchen, where it was warm and my clothes were dry. My wardrobe was complete, even to my shoes, for I had not removed anything when I went overboard. The landlady had kept the fire going all night and had dried all our apparel, but as the other three were not going out as early as I was she gave mine the preference, and I left the house feeling warm and comfortable.

As I walked down from our little hotel I shall never forget that beautiful morning in the quaint old town of Queenstown. The sun was shining warmly, and hardly a breath of air was stirring. As the day grew older and the people who had been rescued turned out into the street, it was as sad a sight as I ever care to see. It was surprising that so many people had removed most of their clothing before taking to the water the day before.

I found many who had no ready cash, and I soon made good use of the English pounds I had bought before I left home. Then I bethought myself of the £40.0.0 draft I had. I had not "crossed" this, so it was good for cash if I could get anybody to cash it. The bank doesn't open at Queenstown until

10 o'clock, and you can bet I was there at ten minutes to. I rang the bell and got inside, took out the still half-soaked draft, endorsed it in the presence of the cashier, handed it in and said I would take the £40.0.0 half in gold and half in paper. He told me he didn't know me; and I told him that didn't make any difference, I didn't know him. He said he couldn't guarantee my signature, but I told him that I thought my signature was as good as his money. I produced my soaked passport and showed him my autograph on that, to compare with that on the draft, and I told him that I had about 12 half-starved, half-naked Americans that had to be fed and clothed, and certainly his big Irish heart wouldn't permit him to refuse to cash an honest draft. I told him I intended to stay right there until I got it; and I did, and I talked to him a steady string, and I didn't get a bit hard-hearted when

he told me he'd probably lose his job if the draft turned out bad. The £40.0.0 was a God-send. I divided it up into as small fractions as possible, and it was able to help out a number of people.

Right here I want to say that the United States consul at Queenstown, Wesley Frost, is a real man, and before noon word had been passed around that Ambassador Page had sent him plenty of funds for all Americans. Perhaps if I had known this money was coming, I wouldn't have given that honest Irish paying teller in the bank such an attack of heart disease.

Then I went back to the "Bar" and my landlady gave me a real breakfast, for I felt that I needed to get stoked up a bit before I took on the unhappy task of viewing the bodies to see if I could identify any of my fellow passengers. It was a hard thing to put through, and I regret to say that it was without satisfactory results, for I found not one that I knew.

In the slip beside the Cunard wharf there were six lifeboats, Nos. 1, 11, 13, 15, 19, and 21; these were all starboard boats, and you will notice what a jump there is between the numbers 1 and 11. As the ship went down by the head, of course it gave more time to clear the after boats which carry the higher numbers. I didn't see one boat successfully cleared from the port side.

I had decided to go through that day to London on the 3 o'clock train and help through the K——'s. McM——, my bedfellow, had found his friend L——, and as he was in good hands and wanted to rest up a bit he decided to stay. There was no chance of getting K—— up on to a jaunting car, he was suffering too much, so I went out into the street and held up a private motor car, for you couldn't hire one in Queenstown, and after a few words of explanation the owner came gladly to the hotel and took Mr. and Mrs. K—— to the station.

We had a comfortable trip to Kingstown and got aboard the Irish mail packet for another little trip on the water. We had telegraphed ahead for a cabin, and we got K—— stretched out in one of the berths and made him as comfortable as we could. He slept from sheer exhaustion. Mrs. K—— and I half sat up on the opposite sofa. Shortly the steamer was under way. It was not what you would call a desirable cabin, for it was directly over the engines and they pounded terrifically; I'll admit that about every throb of the engines went through the pit of my stomach, but finally I dozed off, for I was pretty much "all in." I must have waked at intervals of ten or fifteen minutes, and on looking out of the corner of my eye at Mrs. K—— I saw one of the most charming pieces of devotion that I have ever witnessed. I am confident she never closed her eyes all night nor did she take them off her husband's face — she just silently watched. I had slept about an hour, when I went up on deck to see what was doing. In passing through the saloon a weird sight met my eyes and one that I am glad the K——'s did not see. Every man who had been a passenger on the Lusitania was sitting by a table or reclining on a couch, with a life-belt strapped around him. Many had the original ones from the Lusitania. It was certainly "a gloom." I went up on deck and that was still more weird. Not a light to be seen; every porthole was heavily curtained and heavy canvas was stretched along the side, and the only thing visible was the masthead light. It was blowing half a gale and we were making 23.8 knots per hour. As I came around the corner from the shelter of the cabin the wind nearly struck me off my feet. The canvas was slatting back and forth with reports like cannon, and I clung to the rail fascinated by this wild dash. Would that the "Lucy" had shown such speed! There was a haze that could almost be called a fog, but no horn was sounded as we tore through the black night. I crawled back to the shelter of the cuddy and there found the second Officer. He was a fine chap and we had a chat in his cabin. That wild dash I shan't forget for one while!

We arrived on time at Holyhead and I found the stateroom on the train for which I had wired. Clad in that famous pair of Irish pajamas, before the train hauled out of the station I was dead to the world. It must have been just about one o'clock A.M. I knew nothing until quarter to seven, when the attendant told me that we would arrive at Euston in 15 minutes. He brought in a dish of tea and some bread and butter. Ye gods, didn't that taste good! I had had no food for twelve hours. I asked him for a repeat order. Then I went back in the train and found the K——'s, and they were quite refreshed and told me not to bother with them longer, as they could manage to get in a taxi as soon as they were dressed. They were going to her parents, who live in London.

I left them for a moment saying that I would return and stepped out on the platform. Euston Station at seven o'clock on a Sunday morning is generally not a lively place, and I didn't think that there would be anyone there, or at least not more than a few people to meet friends. I hadn't stepped a foot from the door of the coach when I was almost mobbed by a bunch of reporters. Talk of *it*. Good heavens, I wanted quiet; I didn't want to be interviewed. I stood perfectly still and never said a word; they must have thought I was tongue-tied. Then a poor old woman pushed her way through and asked me, with tears in her eyes, if I had seen "Johnny Keene." How could I answer her? From her appearance I judge he must have been a stoker or in the third cabin. I told her as gently as I could that I hadn't seen him, but many others were coming through in the second and third sections and he might be among them. When the reporters found they couldn't get anything out of me they cleared out, and I was surrounded by friends and relatives of the passengers, who asked me a dozen questions, but I couldn't give any cheerful answers. My nerve wasn't any too good for this ordeal, and I was fast breaking down when a young man pushed through and asked me if I was an American. When I told him "Yes" he said that he was secretary to Ambassador Page, and was there anything he could do for me. I almost fell on his neck with joy, and he took me down to where the Ambassador was standing and introduced me to him. It was a pleasure to hear Ambassador Page say, "What, not the son of *the* Mr. Lauriat of Boston"! So you see, my father, your name is not without honour in your own city. The Ambassador's sympathy was warmly expressed, and he was putting me into the Embassy motor car — for I didn't care where I went as long as I got away from that station platform—when I saw Mr. Walford coming down the platform. I excused myself and stopped him.

I had wired Mr. Walford (our resident London agent) before leaving Queenstown, asking him to meet me if convenient and to have a taxi. I knew that he lived far out in the suburbs, and that if he were not forewarned there would be no way of his getting to the station on Sunday morning. Previously in the day (Saturday) when I had wired him to cable you, I had added the words that I would wire my plans later in the day. This second wire which I sent from Queenstown did not reach him, although he waited at his shop until 8 o'clock Saturday night.

He had decided that if there was any way of getting directly through to London that I would come. So he set his clock for 4 A.M., got up, made himself a cup of tea, and walked from his house to Euston, a distance of 9 miles—that's some demonstration of friendship!

He insisted that I come to his house, and I certainly wanted to do so, for his home looked better to me than the Hotel Kingsley or the Embassy. I took Mr. Walford back to the Ambassador and introduced him. On explaining the situation to Mr. Page he told me by all means to follow my own wishes.

We arrived at the home in the suburbs and Mrs. Walford was there to give me a hearty welcome. I must have been a "sad sketch" as I walked into their hospitable home. I had no hat, for I hadn't spent the time to get one at Queenstown and I knew I had one here in London. I hadn't had a comb in my hair since I got up Friday noon. All my worldly possessions were in a small "brown-paper parcel" tucked under my arm; so even Ben Franklin didn't have much on me when he struck Philadelphia in the old days, as the story goes.

After breakfast they tucked me into bed with a-big-fat-hot-water-bottle, and after a few hours' sleep under that hospitable roof I was quite myself again. A hot tub and shave put on the final touches.

Monday morning, despite their kind invitation to stay with them as long as I wished, I felt I ought to take up my abode at the Hotel

Kingsley and commence picking up the threads of business, although I knew I should feel pretty much lost when I had not a single memorandum "to get on with." My small leather case containing all my business papers had gone down with the Lusitania. Think of a "Lauriat" trying to do business without a lot of neat little folders sitting around his desk!

I shall follow with keen interest the Official Inquiry to be held by Lord Mersey, for I want to see if these points are brought out:—

1. What were the instructions from the Admiralty for the navigation of the ship and were they carefully followed out?

2. Why were we not running top speed?

3. Why were the portholes on decks D open? Never mind the "why," but I should like to have the fact established as to whether they were or were not open.

4. WHY did Captain Turner and Captain Anderson give orders to the crew to "Stop lowering the boats" on the port side and for the passengers "to get out of the boats"? That is the exact phraseology they used. It seemed to me that boats on the port side should have been lowered *at once* as the more the steamer listed the less possible it would be to clear them.

There are three suggestions I shall hope to see put before the Board that are based on the experiences of the catastrophe. They are:—

1. The thing that impressed me most as the people rushed back and forth on the steamer was that more than half of those who had on life jackets had them on incorrectly. I should like to see recommended to the Board that a *law* (international, if possible) be passed, that when a person buys a steamship ticket for a transatlantic crossing, no matter for what class, he or she shall

be obliged to put on a sample life jacket, which shall always be kept in the main offices of the steamship company and in the offices of all their agents, and that the prospective passenger shall be obliged to put it on, fasten it to him, and walk around the office four or five times until he gets familiar with the touch of it and knows how to put it on correctly. It is all very well to hang up neat little signs in the staterooms telling passengers how to put them on and showing where the jackets are, but from what I saw on the Lusitania I don't believe one person in fifty follows these suggestions.

Of course I can hear the steamship companies remonstrate and say that this suggestion is inconvenient, impracticable, etc., etc.; but as long as people cross the ocean there will be such disasters as the Titanic and the Empress of Ireland, but we hope never again such a tragedy as the Lusitania.

If it is convenient for the prospective passenger to put on the life jacket, his ticket should be so stamped with some large distinctive mark as to show that he has complied with the law. Those who have not tried on the life jacket should *not* have the ticket stamped; but immediately after leaving port, when the tickets are collected, they should be examined, and all those passengers who have not complied with the law shall be looked out by an officer and then instructed as to where the life jackets are in the staterooms and how to put them on. Certainly in this way people would become familiar with the sight and touch of a life jacket, and in a disaster, the passenger would be spared that additional shock that comes to the stoutest heart when one puts it on for the first time — plus the existing necessity.

2. I should like to see recommended

that large chests of life belts be kept on the upper decks, for in a catastrophe like that of last Friday it was impossible for some people to go below to get life belts. They had neither the time nor the courage. We could have helped a lot and saved more if we had had more life belts at hand that we could have tied on to the passengers.

3. These collapsible boats should be opened on the deck during each passage of the steamer, and it should be assured that the metal running gear is thoroughly greased and runs smoothly. There should be *some oars* in the boat, for had there been a sea on when this catastrophe happened, of what earthly use would this boat have been without an oar with which even to steer? Under the conditions in which we worked it was easy enough to get oars, but we never could have got them if it had been at all rough.

PART II

PART II

THE foregoing is the crude Narrative practically verbatim as I sent it home to my people. My first thought was to rewrite it and embody it in the following, but I prefer to let it stand as I gave it to the typist in our London office, reciting the tale to her as the events, still vivid in my mind, passed mentally before me.

In this second part I have tried to round out the Narrative by adding details which would answer questions arising from reading Part One.

On boarding the Lusitania on May 1 in New York I found the usual company of passengers and many friends to bid them "bon voyage." I was surprised that access to the steamer was allowed so freely. The two members of my family who accompanied me were allowed to pass aboard without question.

NOTICE!

TRAVELLERS intending to embark on the Atlantic voyage are reminded that a state of war exists between Germany and her allies and Great Britain and her allies; that the zone of war includes the waters adjacent to the British Isles; that, in accordance with formal notice given by the Imperial German Government, vessels flying the flag of Great Britain, or of any of her allies, are liable to destruction in those waters and that travellers sailing in the war zone on ships of Great Britain or her allies do so at their own risk.

IMPERIAL GERMAN EMBASSY.

WASHINGTON, D. C., April 22, 1915.

Naturally I saw the notice issued by the Imperial German Embassy, published in all of the New York papers of May 1. On the opposite page I reprint the whole notice issued by the Embassy in order to correct the erroneous impression I find held by many people, that the Lusitania was specified in it.

It is a coincidence that this notice appeared in some of the New York papers beside the advertisement of the proposed sailings of the Cunard Line. Like many other passengers I gave the notice no serious thought. No idea of cancelling my trip occurred to me. I did not sail with a feeling of defiance towards the Embassy, either for the notice or for any action that might follow; but I admit that I did not think any human being with a drop of red blood in his veins, called a man, could issue an order to sink a passenger steamer without at least giving the women and children a chance to get away.

True, it was a ship of a belligerent nation and carried citizens of countries with which Germany was at war, but I could not believe their policy of "frightfulness" would be carried to such an extent as events afterwards proved. The steamer did have in her cargo some ammunition, but taking all things into consideration I did not believe an order would be given to torpedo this boat without warning, and without an opportunity being given to passengers to take to the boats, and so possibly cause one of the greatest marine disasters of modern times. The order is now a proven fact in history.

We had a pleasant crossing, smooth seas, with sunshine and very little fog.

I enjoyed roaming about the boat exceedingly, as I had never before taken passage on one of the "greyhounds," although it was my twenty-third crossing. I always enjoy the voyage and prefer a smaller and slower boat; but this year I wanted to make my business trip as short as possible, and had the Lusitania gone through at her usual rate of speed and arrived at Liverpool as scheduled, I could have taken up my work the following Saturday morning.

As the days passed the passengers seemed to enjoy them more and more, and formed those acquaintances such as one does on an ocean crossing. Each evening, in the smoking room, the pool for the following day's run was auctioned, and that always makes for informality and companionship.

Thursday evening the usual concert was given and much enjoyed.

Friday morning early there was some fog, but I arose at eight as usual and had my sea bath. As the horn was blowing and the weather was thick, I returned to my berth for a few hours' extra snooze. I instructed the steward that if he didn't hear from me by 12 o'clock he was to call me, as that would give me ample time to get ready for lunch at one.

At noon he came and told me that we had picked up Cape Clear and had put the clock one hour and forty minutes ahead to Greenwich time. I got up and dressed, and was on deck at about ten minutes to one for a short stroll before lunch. It was a beautiful day then, light wind, a smooth sea, and bright sunshine. I thought to myself that if a German submarine really meant business, she would have to wait weeks for a more ideal chance than the present weather conditions. With a flat, unbroken sea, such as that around us, the periscope of a submarine could certainly carry a long distance. On the port side was the good old Irish Coast, and it seemed to me that we were going up the old beaten track that ocean liners have taken for the last fifty years. I was surprised that we were following it, but I was more than surprised at the slow speed we were making. There was no use of one asking questions of the officers, for we all knew they were told to discreetly hold their tongues.

I went down to lunch at one o'clock and finished shortly before two.

The portholes along both sides of the dining saloon were open. I had special reason to notice this, as my seat was directly under an electric fan, and several times on the voyage when the portholes were open and the fan going the draught was so strong that I had been obliged to request the steward to shut off the fan. This was the case this noon.

My table companion was Lothrop Withington. We had a jolly time together and made plans for seeing each other in London, as his rooms were near our London office.

Poor chap, I wish I had seen him after we were struck, that I might have given him a helping hand.

After luncheon I left the saloon, went to my stateroom and then up on deck and joined the Hubbards on the port side. Immediately after the explosion the ship took a sharp list to the starboard and a decided pitch by the head. You could feel the two separate motions very distinctly. It seemed as if she were going down at once, but then she stopped suddenly as if the sea had met the water-tight bulkheads and she seemed to right herself and even raise her bow a little. This gave me a feeling of security, and I at first thought she would stay afloat. As soon as the ship found herself I looked over the rail and made a mental note as to how far she had rolled out.

From the moment we were struck no sense of fear or doubt entered my mind but

RMS *Lusitania* bow and portside in harbor (Library of Congress)

Lusitania at the Liverpool dock (Mike Poirier collection)

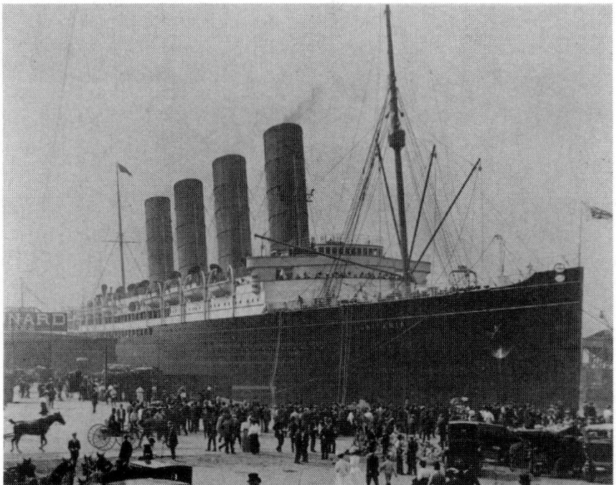

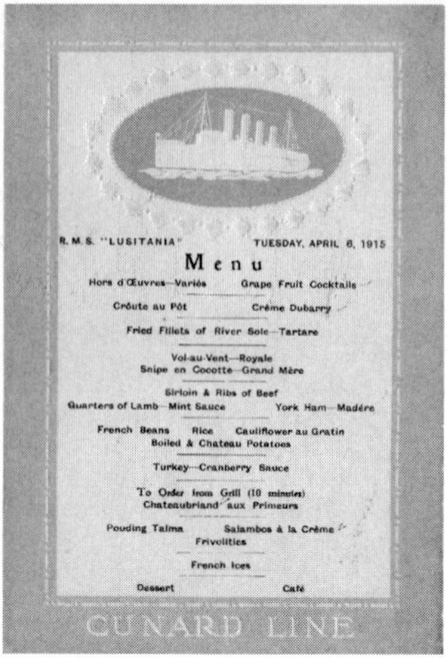

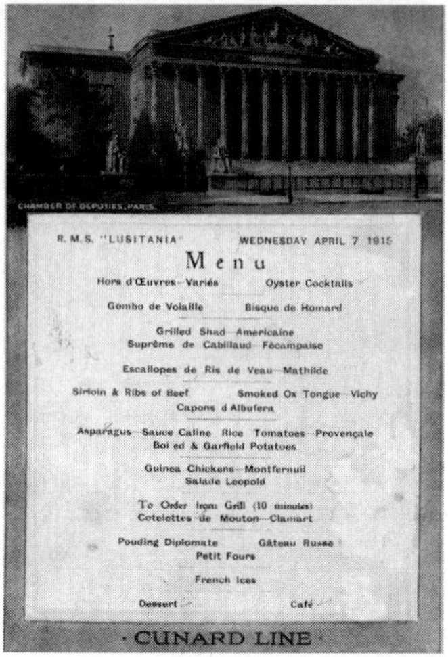

First class menus dated April 6 and April 7, 1915 (Mike Poirier collection)

Album pages from the *Lusitania*'s last safe crossing, April 17-24, 1915 (Mike Poirier collection)

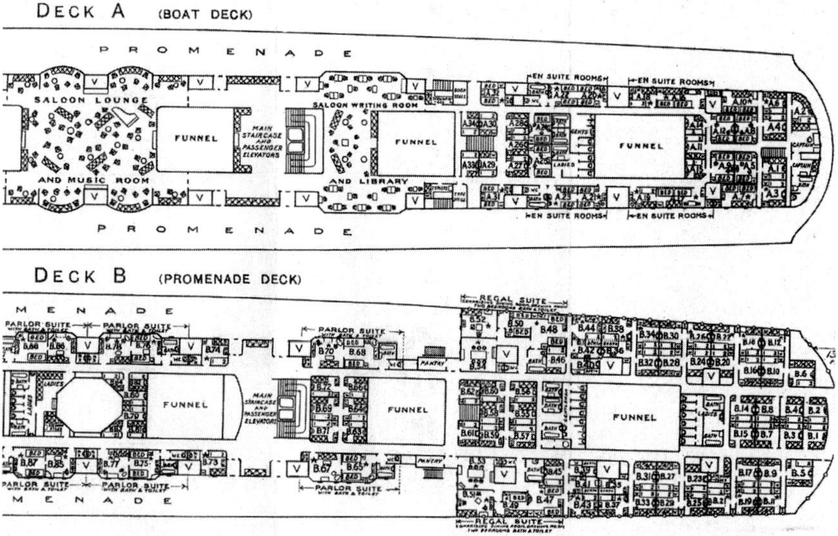

A brochure deck plan showing A and B deck to potential passengers. Lauriat's cabin is the furthest forward, B-5 (Mike Poirier collection)

Lusitania's first class promenade on B deck. Same deck as Lauriat's cabin, B-5 (Mike Poirier collection)

William Thomas Turner, captain of the RMS *Lusitania* when it sank (Library of Congress)

Drawing shows the *Lusitania* as a second torpedo hits behind a gaping hole in the hull (Library of Congress)

B. amd Wm. Gardner, brothers rescued from the *Lusitania*, May 24, 1915 (Library of Congress)

Woman rescued, May 25 (Library of Congress)

American victims of the *Lusitania* (Library of Congress)

THE BOSTON GLOBE—SATURDAY, MAY 8, 1915

ON LUSITANIA AFTER MARRIAGE IN BOSTON

Mr and Mrs Stewart S. Mason Were on Way to Live in Suffolk, Eng.

MRS STEWART SOUTHAM MASON.

Bride, Who Was Miss Leslie Hawthorne Lindsey, Formerly Gave Dancing Exhibitions.

THREE FROM LOWELL.

CAPT SECCOMBE'S CHILDREN

SEVERAL RHODE ISLANDERS.

OPERA HOUSE ARTIST.

AUTHOR OF "THE HYPHEN."

LOTHROP WITHINGTON.

SOME WELL-KNOWN MEN WHO SAILED ON THE LUSITANIA

CHARLES KLEIN.

ALFRED G. VANDERBILT.

ELBERT HUBBARD.

D. A. THOMAS.

CHARLES FROHMAN.

ON WAY TO IDENTIFY WIFE.

NOTABLE BUSINESS MEN ON LUSITANIA

S. M. Knox, W. S. Hodges and H. J. Keser in List.

Steel Manufacturers Went Abroad to Close War Contracts.

PITTSBURG MANUFACTURERS.

EX-CANADIAN MINISTER.

MRS VANDERBILT ANXIOUS.

DOUBLE LIFE IS CHARGED

Two Claim to Be Widow of Leach.

Tangle Follows Railway Man's Death in Worcester.

Never Divorced, Roxbury Woman Declares.

ONLY WIDOW, SHE SAYS.

HAS MAN IN VIEW FOR ROURKE'S PLACE

Mayor Refuses Offer From Henry Welles Durham.

New Yorker Says City Should Spend $27,500,000 for Streets.

Land Takings Approved.

Finds No One Sustained Damages.

GEORGE H. WHALLEY DEAD.

BOY KILLED IN A FIST FIGHT

Mitchell J. Allan of East Boston Dead.

Henry Paraboschi Held on a Charge of Manslaughter.

Youths Adjourned to Lot to Settle School Row.

MITCHELL J. ALLAN.

DEFEATS PRINCETON.

DIVES THROUGH WINDOW.

Early coverage of the tragedy from the *Boston Globe*—Saturday, May 8, 1915

Lauriat's story, noted in the *Boston Globe*—Monday, June 28, 1915

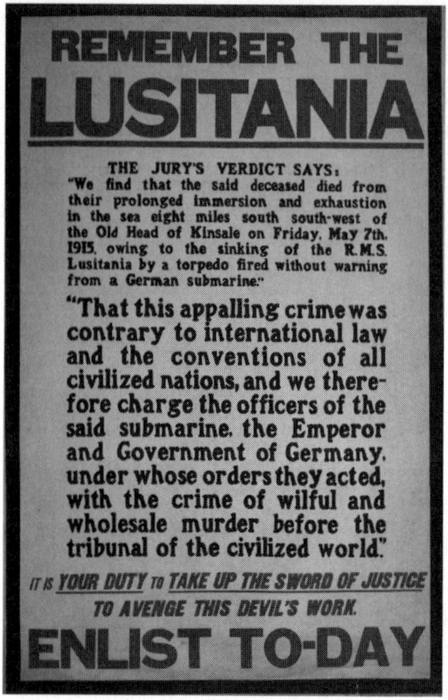

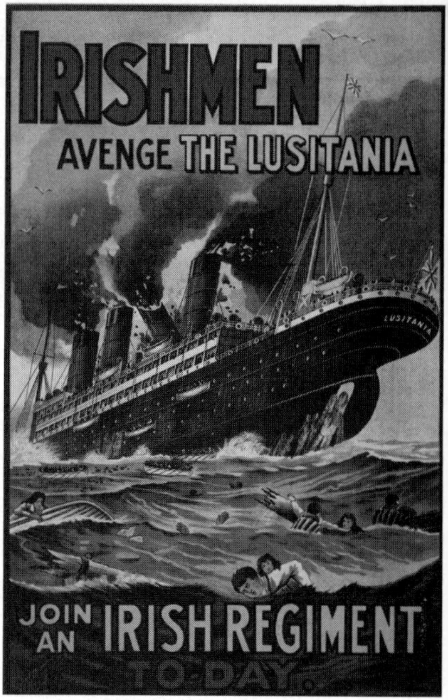

The sinking of the *Lusitania* inspired recruitment efforts for the war (Library of Congress)

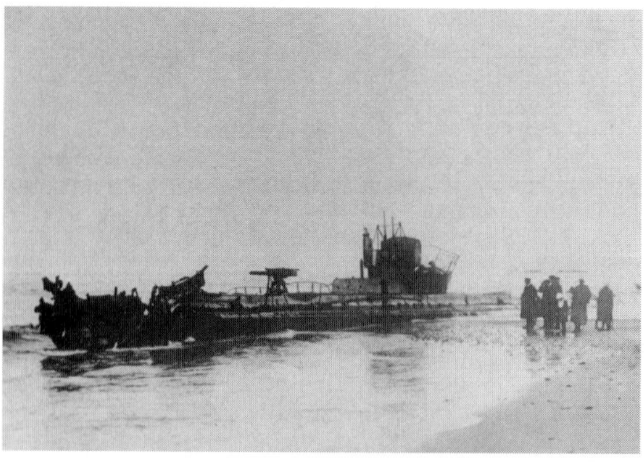

German submarine *U-20* on the Danish coast, said to be the one that sank *Lusitania* (Library of Congress)

that I could perfectly well save myself. If she did sink I could step into the water, and I was confident that I could paddle round for several hours until I was rescued. My experience had been such that a few hours more or less in the water made no difference to me, and I didn't care particularly whether it was a swim in the Irish Sea or Hull Bay.

I spoke to the Hubbards, but when they showed no inclination to go to their cabin to get their life jackets I tapped Mr. Hubbard on the shoulder to emphasize the following remark, "If you don't care to come, stay here and I will get them for you." It did not take me many minutes to go to my cabin, get several life jackets, which I strung on my arm, take my small leather case which contained my business papers, and return to the spot where I had left the Hubbards. I wish with all my heart that they had waited until I came back. If only they had . . . ! But I must not write about the "ifs" of this catastrophe. They would in themselves make a book larger than the account of the disaster itself.

I stood there a few moments hoping the Hubbards would return. I put on to women all but two of the life jackets, for these I felt I should keep for a few moments to see if my friends returned.

Passengers were already crowding on the deck, running back and forth, and as I walked aft I saw no officer taking charge of the lowering of any one lifeboat, but there were attempts being made by the crew to lower two or three of the boats. As early as this in the catastrophe there was confusion, and nothing seemed to be done with usual ship's discipline.

If the passengers, when they first came on deck, had found that the officer and the crew of each lifeboat were at their station, waiting or taking orders from the bridge, it would have inspired confidence and saved the immediate confusion; but there was no such discipline.

I had walked fore and aft on the deck once or twice, stopping often to help people put on their life jackets correctly, when Captain Turner gave his order not to lower the boats.

So insistent was Captain Turner that this order should be carried out that he sent Captain Anderson, who was on the bridge at the time, down along the port side, where I was standing, to enforce it.

As soon as Captain Turner gave this order, the crew, who were on the deck above lowering the boats, immediately took a couple of turns around the cleats and naturally left for parts unknown; at least I did not see them go back to their posts.

Then Captain Turner went down to the

starboard end of the bridge, and I could hear him call out to clear away and lower the boats, meaning those on that side. To me these two orders have always seemed most inconsistent.

The incident that stands out most clearly in my mind up to this time is my meeting an Italian family, consisting of an aged woman, probably the grandmother, the mother, and her three children. They beseeched me in their native tongue, but not a word could I understand. They were third cabin passengers and had found their way to deck B in remarkably quick time.

By this time I had given up hope of seeing the Hubbards again, so I put the two remaining life jackets on the two older women and got another for the oldest child. They were all calm and sat down on one of the collapsible lifeboats, quietly awaiting instructions as to what to do next. As I look back on that family sitting there on the deck it is one of the most pathetic things I remember. One felt so helpless. The boats were not being lowered, and there was absolutely nothing you could do to save a family like this.

It was then I looked over the side and made up my mind that the steamer, rolling out at the angle which she had reached, with the bow under water, could not float much longer, so I started on my second trip to my stateroom.

I tried to go down by the main companion-way, but it was full of people making their way up. It was not so crowded but that I could have forced my way through, but to have done so would only have added to the confusion already paramount, so I went down by the for'ard companion-way.

On my way back from my stateroom I made up my mind that the boat was going to sink. I had thought so before, but I was confident of it after that second trip down. The part of the boat where my stateroom was located was in darkness. The portholes at the bottom of the cross passages which I passed were open, and naturally very little light came through them, as they were only a few feet from the water and the list of the steamer had shut out the direct daylight so there was only the reflection from the water.

On my return, I did not at first go up the for'ard companion-way. I went along the passage to the main companion-way, as I knew I could be of assistance in helping someone up the stairs. By that time there was a jam. Many people found difficulty in climbing the sloping stairs, and so I spoke to several and led them back along the passage I had just come through and up the for'ard companion-way. That at least got them on deck, even though I could not do anything for them after that.

Without thinking, I made my way back to the spot where I was standing with the Hubbards when the explosion occurred. It was curious that I kept coming back to this part of the deck. I must have returned there more than a half dozen times, led back instinctively, I suppose, by the hope that I might find my friends.

It was at this spot that I looked over the side when she was first struck, and where I stood each time I wanted to see how far she had rolled out. A glance for'ard showed me how far she had sunk by the head.

As I looked up and down the deck wild confusion had broken loose. Frantic efforts were at last being made to lower the lifeboats, but as they had been originally swung clear of the steamer, the acute list which she had now taken to starboard caused many of the davits on the port side to swing inboard so far, that it was humanly impossible to push out the boats clear of the edge of the deck. There was nothing more one could do on the port side to help on, so I stepped inside of the main entrance, and slid across to the starboard side.

As I came out I noticed a lifeboat just getting away. It was one that had swung on the davits opposite the main entrance. The water was then almost flush with the scuppers of deck B. I tried to walk aft on the starboard side, but there was such infinite confusion that I saw I could be of no help. Most of the passengers had gone to that side, and as the bow settled and the water rose on the deck they naturally crowded aft, up to the higher part of the deck. All were doing the best they could, but there was no discipline or order.

Personally I didn't care to get into a lifeboat. I was perfectly willing to take my chance in the water, but as I returned to the for'ard part of the deck I saw a sight that simply demanded action on my part.

I found myself opposite the stern of a boat, into which had climbed about thirty-five people, principally women and children. The for'ard davit was about a foot from the bow, and at the rate the Lusitania was going down it meant but a few moments before the bow of the boat would be caught by the davit, and this whole boatload would be taken down, or at least thrown violently into the water.

I judge that this particular boat in the first rush had been lowered many feet to the water and as the steamer sank she floated, and so the distance between the lifeboat and the davits gradually shortened. The slack of the ropes had to fall somewhere and as the ropes fouled on themselves in the bow and the stern of the boat, it convinces me that there was no way on the steamer.

Certainly one ought to make the attempt to clear this boat and not let those women and children be drowned without an effort to save them. Someone was working on the bow ropes, so I climbed into the stern and threw clear my end, but before I had time to cast off the block it was done for me by a seaman who had stepped into the boat apparently at the same moment that I had. My next thought was of the for'ard ropes. I looked and saw someone struggling to clear them. As I have written, I think he was a steward, cutting at them with a knife. I yelled to him to take the axe. He looked around a moment and said there was none. I looked in my end and found none. Then I stepped up on the seat, planning to go for'ard to see if I could help. As I straightened up to get my balance, my back came in contact with the davit hanging over the after end. The blow knocked me down into the bottom of the boat. Then I tried again, looking out for the davit and stepping from one seat to the next. I couldn't avoid the oars, of which there seemed an infinite number. I stepped on one which rolled over. Again I slipped to the bottom of the boat. When I got up and looked for'ard I saw it was too late to make a further attempt, for the end of the davit had gripped the bow of the boat and had just begun to press it under.

I turned to the people and told them to jump. It was their only chance. I begged them to! One or two men did, and finally two women who had on life jackets. When I saw them go I felt that I could be of use to them, so I stepped over and pushed them ahead of me as I swam. A short distance out I found a third woman. They all three kept calm, and I was able to get them to put their hands on each others' shoulders, two in front and one behind.

I stopped swimming for a moment, telling them to wait, for I wished to turn around and see how near the steamer was to her final plunge. I felt that there would be considerable suction, and I wanted to try and keep the three women out of it.

The steamer had an acute list to starboard, so as I looked back I could clearly see the people on deck B, clinging to the rail that ran along the side of the house. It was impossible to stand on the deck unless one had hold of some stationary object. People were clinging to one another, so that it seemed as if they were standing three or four abreast by the rail. As the steamer sank by the head and the water rose higher up the deck, those in front were obliged to release their hold.

It was a terrifying sight for the people back of them, but there were no hysterical shrieks. The men, women, and children on that steamer met their end like heroes, every one of them.

It was at this point that the aërial caught me and took me down. I couldn't imagine what was landing on me out of the sky. I wouldn't have been as much surprised if the submarine had risen and I had found myself on her, but to get a bolt from the blue did surprise me. I shook this off my head and so got a glimpse of what it was that struck me. I saw it was one of the aërials, but fortunately it was the outside one, so I knew the other was between me and the steamer. As the three women were out beyond me they were safe from both aërials. This wire took me rapidly under, but I rose before the steamer sank.

As she went under the sea I was not conscious of hearing cries; rather it was a long, lingering moan that rose, and which lasted for many moments after she disappeared. They who were lost seemed to be calling from the very depths.

I kept my eyes on the steamer until she went out of sight. Then the deluge of wreckage was upon us. That separated me from the women, and I am not confident that I got them afterwards into my boat, but I am quite sure that they must have been saved. They had every chance.

Just before the steamer sank she seemed to right herself and go down on quite an even keel. She settled by the stern, and that is another reason that convinces me that if her portholes had been closed she might have stayed afloat after her bow struck bottom.

Much to my surprise there was only slight suction. There were explosions out of the funnels as the cold water mixed with the steam and that added to the horror of the disaster. The mass of wreckage was tremendous. Aside from the people brought out with it, there were deck chairs, oars, boxes, and I can't remember what. I simply know that one moment one was jammed between large objects, and the next moment one was under the water. There were many people around you who needed assistance, but all one could do was to push an oar or box or a piece of wreckage to each to grab. A few moments after the first rush was over I looked around to see if I could find a boat. A few yards away I saw a collapsible lifeboat floating peacefully around, right side up. I made good time crossing the intervening space and was the first man on that boat. A sailor immediately followed, then G——, and we three got to work opening it up.

When we got the canvas covering off and saw no oars in that boat I was, to say the least, disgusted with any Board of Trade or committee of men who would pass a boat that was worthy to be called one, without deeming it necessary to have her fitted with oars. If there had been a sea on we should have been helpless.

After we got the boat manned and went back into the wreckage it was simply awful. We took those whom we could help, but there were many, many past human assistance. We loaded our little boat to the full limit of its capacity and started for the fishing smack.

As we left with our boatload, I looked around for other boats. There were already two lifeboats between us and the fishing smack; one halfway there and the other about quarter of the way, and there was also one headed toward Kinsale. There was a fourth headed west, apparently rowing for a streak of smoke one could see on the horizon. There must have been at least two lifeboats that stayed at the scene of the wreck doing their utmost.

When we reached the fishing smack the first two lifeboats I have mentioned, had already arrived and had put their human freight aboard. One, in charge of a boatswain, with four of the ship's regular crew rowing, was starting back.

I can't understand why these two lifeboats got away so quickly from the scene of the disaster. It seems to me that they should have stayed right there and taken in more people. There were only about 50 people on the fishing smack, and so that was all the two regular lifeboats brought down. They could have put 75 or 80 people in each one of those boats in perfect safety, the sea was so smooth. There were several remaining hours of daylight in which they could have been picked up, so there was no need to hurry away. Aside from the people they could have taken into the boat, they could have been of much assistance in letting others cling to the sides. There are life lines for just that purpose.

Nearly all of the people that got aboard the fishing smack before us were dry, as these two boats had cleared before the steamer sank. All of the people on my boat had been fished out of the ocean.

About one half an hour after we were aboard the fishing smack another collapsible boat came alongside and we took these people on board.

There were a father and mother and a little year-old baby on the fishing smack. They were fortunate in getting away in one of the lifeboats, and the little chap was one of the few babies who was saved. I have seen it stated that of about 150 children aboard, only about 25 were saved. I can believe that from what I saw when we were back in the wreckage pulling out people.

The trip up on the Flying Fish was uneventful. Many got quite dried off in the engine room and nearly all regained much of their normal composure. There were comparatively few who were in dire distress.

The illustration opposite this page shows the lifeboats as I found them in the slip beside the Cunard wharf on Saturday morning. I called the attention of the newspaper men who had cameras to these boats, and I was glad to see them take the picture. If they hadn't done so I should have had it done, for to me this is a very pretty piece of evidence. The picture reproduced here is taken from one of the London dailies.

I think it would be well for the Cunard Line to explain how lifeboats that are supposed to hold people, should be brought into port carrying so much dunnage.

Look at the oars and sails that were left in these boats, occupying space that could have been better used for carrying human freight! I climbed through each one of these boats, and they all showed evidence of having been used by survivors. You will notice that some of the boats are stripped of all extra fittings, and these probably carried their proper quota of human freight. There are but five of the boats in this picture; the sixth was in another slip.

Evidence has been given that the first torpedo crippled the engines so that it was impossible to reverse the screws and bring the steamer to a stop or slow her down to a point where the captain judged it safe to lower the boats. All right, if that is the opinion of an experienced seaman I shall not dispute it; but I should like to have a naval engineer estimate how much way there could have been on the steamer, say ten minutes after she was struck, even if the engine room wasn't able to reverse the screws and bring her to a stop.

The Lusitania was of 32,000 tons displacement. She was going through the water at about 17 knots an hour. If you suddenly shut off that propulsion, giving her a list to starboard and a rapid settling by the head, I can't believe she would be ranging ahead very fast after the first 10 or 12 minutes.

PART III

PART III

One who has read this Narrative cannot help but being interested in the following account, taken from the "Frankfurter Zeitung" of Sunday, May 9, 1915, issued two days after the tragedy.

I saw several German papers of about that date, but I selected this as a representative one. This article is much saner than others I saw, and I feel gives a fairer idea of what the German press published at that time.

I print the German text, that those who can read it may judge for themselves, and on the opposite page I have given the English translation.

For the transposition of the original German into Roman characters and the translation into English, I am indebted to my friend Ernest F. Langley, Professor of Romance Languages at the Massachusetts Institute of Technology.

If one refers to the reproduction of the plan of the ship, he will see the places indicated where the twelve guns were to have been mounted had the British Government ever taken the Lusitania for an "auxiliary cruiser." While this plan was originally published when the Lusitania was first launched in 1906, it was used again at this time with the position of the guns still showing.

EXTRACTS

WITH TRANSLATIONS FROM THE

"FRANKFURTER ZEITUNG"

FRANKFURTER ZEITUNG

Sonntag, 9 Mai 1915. Was haben wir getan? Ein deutsches Kriegsschiff hat an der Küste Irlands die "Lusitania" vernichtet. Ein gewaltiger Wert, der gegen uns auf der Wagschale des Feindes lag, ist zerstört. Viele Millionen an materiellem Gut sind vernichtet, und ein unermessbarer Besitz an moralischer Kraft und an Gefühlswert eines Volkes, dessen ganzes Leben auf das Blühen seiner Schiffahrt und seines Handels eingestellt ist, sank mit dem stolzen Schiff zu Grunde. Dieses Seevolk ist in seinem Heiligsten getroffen worden. Alle Massregeln seiner Vorsicht waren umsonst. Die deutsche Waffe hat die Schutzwehr durchschnitten. England sieht sich an dieser Stelle nackt und hilflos und ausserstande, mit dem

Sunday, May 9, 1915. What have we done? A German war vessel has sunk the Lusitania off the coast of Ireland. A mighty asset which lay on the enemy's side of the scale is destroyed. Property to the value of many millions is annihilated, and an immeasurable store of moral power and self-confidence of a people whose whole life is centered in the prosperity of its shipping and commerce sank to the bottom with the proud vessel. This maritime nation has been stricken in its Holy of Holies. All measures dictated by its prudence were in vain. Germany's weapon has cut through its armor. England sees herself naked and helpless at this spot and unable to keep pace with her German opponent. Nothing of hypocrisy or

deutschen Gegner Schritt zu halten. Nichts von Heuchelei und Krämergeist! Das Gefühl ist echt. Ohnmächtige Wut! Und das ist es eben, woher uns die Gefahr kam, das ist im letzten Ende auch der Grund, der uns den Krieg gebracht hat: *England*,[1] das Volk zur See, die Weltmacht, ist *eingeholt* von uns Jüngeren, und es gibt Dinge, durch die wir ihm vorangehen. Und weil dies so ist, weil alles schmähliche Verleumden nichts anderes als kraftlose Schläge zur Abwehr sind, Kriegswaffen Englands, nicht von anderer Art als das sinnlose Einsperren der Zivilgefangenen, als die Vergeltungswut gegen die gefangenen U-Bootsleute — darum ist uns dies alles so verächtlich und reizt den Zorn unseres Volkes.

Die "Lusitania" trug *Passagiere!* Wir hätten es wahrhaftig unendlich lieber ge-

[1] Italics are used in the above text where the original German type emphasizes by spacing.

shopkeeper-spirit about it! The feeling is genuine. Impotent rage! And that was the very thing which caused our danger, and, in the last analysis, that also was the reason why war was brought upon us. *England,*[1] the nation of sailors, the world power, *is overtaken* by us juniors, and things exist which enable us to outstrip her. And because this is so, because all her despicable calumny is nothing else than impotent blows to defend herself, typical English weapons, exactly on a par with the senseless confinement of civilians and the fierce reprisals upon the captured submarine crews—because this is so, the whole matter is contemptible in our eyes and provokes the anger of our people.

The Lusitania carried *passengers!* In truth we should have been infinitely better

[1] Italics are used in the translations where the original German text emphasizes by spacing,

sehen, wenn das Schiff, das schon seit vielen Monaten dem Feind von Nutzen ist und uns Schaden bringt, hätte vernichtet werden können, ohne dass diese Katastrophe für seine Fahrgäste hätte kommen müssen. Aber müssen wir uns, denen der Feind das Messer in die Kehle stossen will, wir, deren *Bezwingung durch den Hunger* und den Mangel an Kriegsgerät so ziemlich alle Welt mit Ruhe als ein unvermeidliches Schicksal mitansehen würde, *müssen* wir uns nicht mit aller Kraft und mit allen Mitteln, die der deutsche Geist erfinden kann und die die Ehre des deutschen Volkes als achtbare Waffen anerkennt, gegen diese furchtbare Gefahr wehren, die uns noch immer bedroht? Haben nicht gerade sie den Kampf bis aufs Messer gepredigt und durch ihre Blockade eröffnet, die jetzt zetern, weil die deutschen Waffen die besseren sind? Oder haben jene ein Recht, *uns* anzuklagen, die ihre Ange-

pleased if the ship, which for many months past has been of aid to the enemy and has done us harm, could have been destroyed without the necessity of this catastrophe befalling its passengers. But must we not, we whose throat the enemy is seeking to cut, we whose *defeat by hunger* and by lack of war material nearly every one would witness complacently as an unavoidable fate, *must* we not defend ourselves from this dreadful danger, which still threatens us, with all our might and with all the means that the German spirit can invent and which the honor of the German people recognizes as legitimate weapons? Were not those who now raise outcries because the German weapons are better than their own the very ones who proclaimed war to the knife and opened it with their blockade? Or have they a right to accuse *us*, those who allowed their friends and relatives to entrust themselves to a ship

hörigen sich einem Schiff anvertrauen liessen, dessen Vernichtung mit aller Klarheit zuvor angekündigt war? Auf ein Schiff, das wie ein *Kreuzer*, stärker als irgend ein deutscher geschützter Kreuzer, mit zwölf 15 Zentimeter-Geschützen ausgerüstet war? Sie haben uns, als wir warnten, verspottet. Sie mögen sich an jene wenden, die das *Verbrechen* begangen haben, zur Fahrt auf einem Kriegsschiff Fahrgäste zu laden.

Berlin, 8. Mai (Priv.-Tel. Ctr. Bln.). Der Eindruck, den die *Vernichtung der "Lusitania"* macht, wird weit über Deutschlands und Englands Grenzen hinausreichen, und man kann ohne weiteres annehmen, dass sich auch *neutrale* Stimmen finden werden, die eifernd den Untergang zahlreicher Passagiere beklagen. Gewiss, jedes Menschenleben ist wertvoll und sein Verlust bedauerlich, aber an den Massnahmen und Kampfformen dieses Weltkrieges gemessen, an den

whose destruction was announced with perfect clearness in advance, to a ship equipped like a *cruiser,* more powerfully than any German protected cruiser, with twelve 15 centimeter guns? They mocked at us when we gave warning. Let them turn to those who committed the *crime* of allowing passengers to travel on a war vessel.

Berlin, May 8. The impression created by the sinking of the Lusitania will extend far beyond the borders of Germany and England, and we may at once assume that *neutral* voices also will arise to deeply deplore the loss of a large number of passengers. Every human life is, of course, valuable, and its loss deplorable, but, measured by the methods of this world war, by the methods introduced by our enemies, forcing us to retaliatory measures in self-defence, the death of non-combatants is a matter of no consequence. The standards observed among

Formen, die unsere Feinde eingeführt und durch sie uns zur Gegenwehr gezwungen haben, kommt es auf den Tod von Nichtkämpfern nicht mehr an. Die Massstäbe, die unter zivilisierten Völkern im Frieden galten, sind zerstört worden, und wer uns mit den Opfern der "Lusitania" kommt, der soll sich erst legitimieren und uns die Frage beantworten, ob er gegeifert und gejammert hat, als *russische Heere auf dem Boden Ostpreussens gebrannt, gemordet und geschändet* haben, kaltblütig und bewusst gegen eine friedliche Bevölkerung, gegen Männer, Frauen und Kinder. Das war so gutes Blut, wie nur irgend eines, das in englischen Schiffen auf dem Wasser schwimmt. Und wer da klagt und Zweifel hegt an der Berechtigung unserer Kampfesführung, den fragen wir, wie er über *Englands Aushungerungskrieg gegen Deutschland* denkt, und ob er uns vielleicht zumutet, uns wehrlos aushungern zu

civilized nations in times of peace have been destroyed, and any one reproaching us for the lives sacrificed on the Lusitania should first justify himself and answer for us the question whether he frothed and fumed when *Russian armies on East Prussian soil* coolly and deliberately *burned, murdered and committed outrage* upon a peaceful population, men, women and children? That blood was as good as any sailing on the ocean in English ships. And if anyone complains and feels doubts about the justification of our war methods, we shall ask him what he thinks about *England's war of starvation against Germany*, and whether he imagines perhaps that it is our purpose to allow ourselves to be starved to submission without acting in self-defence? And we shall also ask him what he thinks about the *shipment of thousands of millions worth of arms and munitions from America,*

lassen. Und den fragen wir, wie er über die *Milliardenlieferungen von Waffen und Munition aus Amerika* denkt, diese Mithilfe, durch die allein den Engländern und Franzosen seit Monaten überhaupt die Fortführung des Krieges ermöglicht worden ist. Der nun versenkte Riesendampfer hat erwiesenermassen grosse Mengen von Kriegsmaterial und Munition an Bord gehabt. Er war ausserdem ein *feindliches Kriegsschiff*, denn er war stark armiert. Er war ein *Hilfskreuzer*. Und zum Dritten fällt ins Gewicht: keine Warnung ist unterblieben, die geeignet war, zu verhindern, dass Passagiere die gewagte Fahrt auf diesem Schiffe unternahmen. Unser *Botschafter* in *Washington* hat in amerikanischen Blättern offiziell vor dieser Fahrt gewarnt. Nur Spott und Hohn in der angesehensten englischen Presse ist die Antwort gewesen. Die Besitzer der "Lusitania" haben vielleicht geglaubt, dass diese

an assistance by which alone, generally speaking, during the past months, the continued participation in the war has been made possible for the English and French. The huge steamer now at the bottom of the ocean had, as has been proved, a great quantity of war material and munitions on board. She was moreover an *enemy's war vessel,* for she was heavily armed. She was an *auxiliary cruiser.* And thirdly it must be considered that no warning calculated to prevent passengers undertaking the perilous voyage on this vessel was neglected. Our *ambassador* at *Washington* gave official warning about this voyage in the American newspapers. Nothing but mockery and scorn was the answer in the most highly respected English press. The owners of the Lusitania believed, perhaps, that these passengers would form a protection for the contraband and the lucrative shipment of

Passagiere ein Schutz für die Kontrebande, für die lohnende Waffenlieferung, die an ihrem Bord waren, bilden würden. Die "Deutsche Tageszeitung" hat recht, wenn sie sagt: "Die an Bord der 'Lusitania' untergegangenen Passagiere sind, wenn man das Ding beim rechten Namen nennen will, ein Opfer grossbritannischer Frivolität und Habsucht."

arms which were on board. The *Deutsche Tageszeitung* is right in saying: "The passengers who went down with the Lusitania are, if we wish to call things by their right names, a sacrifice to Great Britain's frivolity and avarice."

PART IV

PART IV

I WROTE parts I and II before reading a word of the Official Inquiry held by Lord Mersey and his Assessors, or even the meagre newspaper accounts of the investigation that were published in the London papers while I was there. I wished to write with an open mind and did not want to know a word of the Court's Findings until I had finished mine.

I held my own little Court of Inquiry, with my own eyes and brain offering the evidence. My findings as written in the first two parts are as diametrically opposite from those of Lord Mersey's Court as they well could be. I have printed mine in full and so I now do the same to his.

LOSS OF THE STEAMSHIP "LUSITANIA"

REPORT of a Formal Investigation into the circumstances attending the foundering on the 7th of May, 1915, of the British Steamship "Lusitania," of Liverpool, after being torpedoed off the Old Head of Kinsale, Ireland.

REPORT OF THE COURT

The Court, having carefully enquired into the circumstances of the above mentioned disaster, finds, that the loss of the said ship and lives was due to damage caused to the said ship by torpedoes fired by a submarine of German nationality whereby the ship sank.

In the opinion of the Court the act was done not merely with the intention of sinking the ship, but also with the intention of destroying the lives of the people on board.

Dated this seventeenth day of July, 1915.

MERSEY,
Wreck Commissioner.

We concur in the above Report,

F. S. Inglefield
H. J. Hearn
David Davies
John Spedding
} *Assessors.*

THE LUSITANIA'S LAST VOYAGE

INTRODUCTION

On the 18th of May, 1915, the Board of Trade required that a Formal Investigation of the circumstances attending the loss of the "Lusitania" should be held, and the Court accordingly commenced to sit on the 15th of June.

There were six sittings, some of which were public and some of which were in camera. Thirty-six witnesses were examined, and a number of documents were produced.

THE SHIP

The "Lusitania" was a Turbine steamship built by John Brown & Co., of Clydebank, in 1907, for the Cunard Steamship Company. She was built under Admiralty Survey and in accordance with Admiralty requirements, and was classed 100 A.1. at Lloyd's. Her length was 755 feet, her beam 88 feet, and her depth 60 feet 4 in. Her tonnage was 30,395 gross and 12,611 net. Her engines were of 68,000 h. p. and her speed 24½ to 25 knots. She had 23 double-ended and two single-ended boilers situated in four boiler-rooms.

The ship was divided transversely by eleven principal bulkheads into twelve sections.

The two forward bulkheads were collision bulkheads without doors. The remaining bulkheads had watertight doors cut in them which were closed by hand. In places where it was necessary to have the doors open for working the ship they could be closed by hydraulic pressure from the bridge. A longitudinal bulkhead separated the side coal bunkers from the boiler-room and engine-rooms on each side of the ship.

The "Lusitania" was a passenger as well as an emigrant ship as defined by the Merchant Shipping Acts. She fulfilled all the requirements of the law in this connection and had obtained all necessary certificates.

She had accommodation on board for 3,000 persons (including the crew).

The Life-Boats and Life-Saving Appliances

The ship was provided with boat accommodation for 2,605 persons. The number of persons on board on the voyage in question was 1,959.

The number of boats was 48. Twenty-two of these were ordinary life-boats hanging from davits—eleven on each side of the boat deck. These had a total carrying capacity of 1,323. The remainder (26) were collapsible boats, with a total carrying capacity of 1,282. Eighteen of these collapsible boats were stowed under eighteen of the life-boats. The remaining eight were stowed four on each side of the ship abaft the life-boats.

In addition the ship was provided with

2,325 life-jackets (125 of which were for children) and 35 life-buoys. All these were conveniently distributed on board.

The boats, the life-jackets and the life-buoys were inspected at Liverpool on the 17th of March, 1915, by the resident Board of Trade Surveyor, and again on the 15th of April, 1915, by the Board of Trade Emigration Officer. Both these gentlemen were called before me and satisfied me that the condition of the different appliances was in every way satisfactory.

The boats were also examined by the ship's carpenter at New York on the commencement of the homeward voyage on the 1st of May and found to be in good order.

The Captain, the Officers and the Crew

The Captain of the ship, Mr. William Thomas Turner, had been in the service of the Cunard Company since 1883. He had occupied the position of Commander since 1903, and had held an Extra Master's Certificate since 1907. He was called before me and gave his evidence truthfully and well. The "Lusitania" carried an additional Captain named Anderson, whose duty it was to assist in the care and navigation of the ship. He was unfortunately drowned when the ship went down, and I can only judge of his capacity, by the accounts given to me of the work he did. Several of the officers gave their evidence before me and gave it well. I am quite satisfied that the two Captains and the officers were competent men, and that they did their duty. Captain Turner remained on the bridge till he was swept into the sea and Captain Anderson was working on the deck until he went overboard and was drowned.

It appears that since the commencement of the war the Cunard Company has lost all its Royal Naval Reserve and Fleet Reserve men, and the managers have had to take on the best men they could get and to train them as well as might be in the time at their disposal. In connection with this training prizes have been given by the Company to induce the crews to make themselves proficient in handling the boats, and the efforts in this direction seem to have been successful in the case of the "Lusitania's" crew. Mr. Arthur Jones, the First Officer, described the crew on this voyage as well able to handle the boats, and testified to their carrying out the orders given to them in a capable manner. One of the crew, Leslie N. Morton, who at the time the ship was torpedoed was an extra look-out on the starboard side of the forecastle head, deserves a special word of commendation. He had been shipped in New York. He was only 18 years of age, but he seems to have exhibited great courage, self-possession and resource. He was the first to observe the approach of the two torpedoes, and before they touched the ship he had reported them to the bridge by means of the megaphone, calling out "Torpedoes coming on the starboard side." When the torpoedoes struck the ship, Morton was knocked off his feet, but, recovering himself quickly, he went at once to the boats on the starboard side and assisted in filling and lowering several of them. Having done all that could be done on board, he had, as he expresses it, "to swim for it." In the water he managed to get hold of a floating collapsible life-boat and, with the assistance of another member of the crew named Parry, he ripped the canvas cover off it, boarded it, and succeeded in drawing into it fifty or sixty passengers. He and Parry rowed the life-boat some miles to a fishing smack, and, having put the rescued passengers on board the smack, they re-entered the life-boat and succeeded in rescuing twenty or thirty more people. This boy, with his mate Parry, was instrumental in saving nearly one hundred lives. He has cause for being proud of the work he did. Morton had a good opportunity of judging how the crew performed their duties in the short time which elapsed between the explosion of the torpedoes and the foundering of the ship. He saw the crew helping the women and children into the boats; he saw them distributing life-belts to the passengers. He heard the officers giving orders and he observed that the crew were obeying the orders properly.

Some of the passengers were called, and they confirm this evidence. They speak in terms of the highest praise of the exertions made by the crew.

No doubt there were mishaps in handling the ropes of the boats and in other such matters, but there was, in my opinion, no incompetence or neglect, and I am satisfied that the crew behaved well throughout, and worked with skill and judgment. Many more than half their number lost their lives.

The total crew consisted of 702, made up of 77 in the Deck Department, 314 in the Engineering Department, 306 in the Stewards' Department and of 5 musicians. Of these, 677 were males and 25 were females. Of the males, 397 were lost, and of the females, 16, making the total number lost, 413. Of the males 280 were saved, and of the females, 9, making the total number saved, 289.

I find that the conduct of the masters, the officers and the crew was satisfactory. They did their best in difficult and perilous circumstances and their best was good.

The Passengers.

The number of passengers on board the "Lusitania" when she sailed was 1,257, consisting of 290 saloon, 600 second-cabin, and 367 third-cabin passengers.

Of these, 944 were British and Canadian, 159 were American, and the remainder were of seventeen other nationalities. Of the British and Canadian 584 perished. Of the American 124 perished, and of the remainder 77 perished. The total number lost was 785, and the total number saved was 472.

The 1,257 passengers were made up of 688 adult males, 440 adult females, 51 male children, 39 female children, and 39 infants. Of the 688 adult males, 421 were lost and 267 were saved. Of the 440 adult females, 270 were lost and 170 were saved. Of the 51 male children, 33 were lost and 18 were saved. Of the 39 female children, 26 were lost and 13 were saved. Of the 39 infants, 35 were lost and 4 were saved.

Many of the women and children among

those lost died from exhaustion after immersion in the water.

I can speak very well of the conduct of the passengers after the striking of the ship. There was little or no panic at first, although later on, when the steerage passengers came on to the boat deck in what one witness described as "a swarm," there appears to have been something approaching a panic.

Some of the passengers attempted to assist in launching the boats and, in my opinion, did more harm than good. It is, however, quite impossible to impute any blame to them. They were all working for the best.

The Cargo

The cargo was a general cargo of the ordinary kind, but part of it consisted of a number of cases of cartridges (about 5,000). This ammunition was entered in the manifest. It was stowed well forward in the ship on the orlop and lower decks and about 50 yards away from where the torpedoes struck the ship. There was no other explosive on board.

The Ship Unarmed

It has been said by the German Government that the "Lusitania" was equipped with masked guns, that she was supplied with trained gunners, with special ammunition, that she was transporting Canadian troops, and that she was violating the laws of the United States. These statements are untrue; they are nothing but baseless inventions, and they serve only to condemn the persons who make use of them. The steamer carried no masked guns nor trained gunners, or special ammunition, nor was she transporting troops, or violating any laws of the United States.

THE LUSITANIA'S LAST VOYAGE

THE VOYAGE

The Departure from New York

The "Lusitania" left New York at noon on the 1st of May, 1915. I am told that before she sailed notices were published in New York by the German authorities that the ship would be attacked by German submarines, and people were warned not to take passage in her. I mention this matter not as affecting the present enquiry but because I believe it is relied upon as excusing in some way the subsequent killing of the passengers and crew on board the ship. In my view, so far from affording any excuse the threats serve only to aggravate the crime by making it plain that the intention to commit it was deliberately formed and the crime itself planned before the ship sailed. Unfortunately the threats were not regarded as serious by the people intended to be affected by them. They apparently thought it impossible that such an atrocity as the destruction of their lives could be in the contemplation of the German Government. But they were mistaken, and the ship sailed.

The Ship's Speed

It appears that a question had arisen in the office of the Cunard Company shortly after the war broke out as to whether the transatlantic traffic would be sufficient to justify the Company in running their two big and expensive ships — the " Lusitania " and the "Mauretania." The conclusion arrived at was that one of the two (the " Lusitania ") could be run once a month if the boiler power were reduced by one-fourth. The saving in coal and labour resulting from this reduction would, it was thought, enable the Company to avoid loss though not to make a profit. Accordingly six of the "Lusitania's" boilers were closed and the ship began to run in these conditions in November, 1914. She had made five round voyages in this way before the voyage in question in this enquiry. The effect of the closing of the six boilers was to reduce the attainable speed from $24\frac{1}{2}$ to 21 knots. But this reduction still left the "Lusitania" a considerably faster ship than any other steamer plying across the Atlantic. In my opinion this reduction of the steamer's speed was of no significance and was proper in the circumstances.

THE TORPEDOING OF THE SHIP

By the 7th of May the "Lusitania" had entered what is called the "Danger Zone," that is to say, she had reached the waters in which enemy submarines might be expected. The Captain had therefore taken precautions. He had ordered all the life-boats under davits to be swung out. He had ordered all bulkhead doors to be closed except such as were required to be kept open in order to work the ship. These orders had been carried out. The portholes were also closed. The lookout on the ship was doubled — two men being sent to the crow's nest and two to the eyes of the ship. Two officers were on the bridge and a quartermaster was on either side with instructions to look out for submarines. Orders were also sent to the engine-room between noon and two P.M. of the 7th to keep the steam pressure very high in case of emergency and to give the vessel all possible speed if the telephone from the bridge should ring.

Up to 8 A.M. on the morning of the 7th the speed on the voyage had been maintained at 21 knots. At 8 A.M. the speed was reduced to 18 knots. The object of this reduction was to secure the ship's arrival outside the bar at Liverpool at about 4 o'clock on the morning of the 8th, when the tide would serve to enable her to cross the bar into the Mersey at early dawn. Shortly after this alteration of the speed a fog came on and the speed was further reduced for a time to 15 knots. A little before noon the fog lifted and the speed was restored to 18 knots, from which it was never subsequently changed. At this time land was sighted about two points abaft the beam, which the Captain took to be Brow Head; he could not, however, identify it with sufficient certainty to enable him to fix the position of his ship upon the chart. He therefore kept his ship on her course, which was S. 87 E. and about parallel with the land until 12:40, when, in order to make a better landfall he altered his course to N. 67 E. This brought him closer to the land, and he sighted the Old Head of Kinsale. He then (at 1:40

P.M.) altered his course back to S. 87° E., and having steadied his ship on that course began (at 1:50) to take a four-point bearing. This operation, which I am advised would occupy 30 or 40 minutes, was in process at the time when the ship was torpedoed, as hereafter described.

At 2 P.M. the passengers were finishing their mid-day meal.

At 2:10 P.M., when ten to fifteen miles off the Old Head of Kinsale, the weather being then clear and the sea smooth, the Captain, who was on the port side of the lower bridge, heard the call, "There is a torpedo coming, sir," given by the second officer. He looked to starboard and then saw a streak of foam in the wake of a torpedo travelling towards his ship. Immediately afterwards the "Lusitania" was struck on the starboard side somewhere between the third and fourth funnels. The blow broke number 5 life-boat to splinters.

A second torpedo was fired immediately afterwards, which also struck the ship on the starboard side. The two torpedoes struck the ship almost simultaneously.

Both these torpedoes were discharged by a German submarine from a distance variously estimated at from two to five hundred yards. No warning of any kind was given. It is also in evidence that shortly afterwards a torpedo from another submarine was fired on the port side of the "Lusitania." This torpedo did not strike the ship, and the circumstance is only mentioned for the purpose of showing that perhaps more than one submarine was taking part in the attack.

The "Lusitania" on being struck took a heavy list to starboard and in less than twenty minutes she sank in deep water. Eleven hundred and ninety-eight men, women, and children were drowned.

Sir Edward Carson, when opening the case, described the course adopted by the German Government in directing this attack as "contrary to International Law and the usages of war," and as constituting, according to the law of all civilized countries, "a deliberate attempt to murder the passengers on board the ship." This statement is, in my opinion, true, and it is made in language not a whit too strong for the occasion. The defenceless creatures on board, made up of harmless men and women, and of helpless children, were done to death by the crew of the German submarine acting under the directions of the officials of the German Government. In the questions submitted to me by the Board of Trade I am asked, "What was the cause of the loss of life?" The answer is plain. The effective cause of the loss of life was the attack made against the ship by those on board the submarine. It was a murderous attack because made with a deliberate and wholly unjustifiable intention of killing the people on board. German authorities on the laws of war at sea themselves establish beyond all doubt that though in some cases the destruction of an enemy trader may be permissible there is always an obligation first to secure the safety of the lives of those on board. The guilt of the persons concerned in the present case is confirmed by the vain excuses which have been put forward on their behalf by the German Government as before mentioned.

One witness, who described himself as a French subject from the vicinity of Switzerland, and who was in the second-class dining-room in the after part of the ship at the time of the explosion, stated that the nature of the explosion was "similar to the rattling of a maxim gun for a short period," and suggested that this noise disclosed the "secret" existence of some ammunition. The sound, he said, came from underneath the whole floor. I did not believe this gentleman. His demeanour was very unsatisfactory. There was no confirmation of his story, and it appeared that he had threatened the Cunard Company that if they did not make him some immediate allowance on account of a claim which he was putting forward for compensation, he would have the unpleasant duty of making his claim in public, and, in so doing, of producing "evidence which will not be to the credit either of your Company or of the Admiralty." The Company had not complied with his request.

It may be worth while noting that Leith, the Marconi operator, was also in the second-class dining-saloon at the time of the explosion. He speaks of but one explosion. In my opinion there was no explosion of any part of the cargo.

THE LUSITANIA'S LAST VOYAGE

Orders Given and Work Done after the Torpedoing

The Captain was on the bridge at the time his ship was struck, and he remained there giving orders until the ship foundered. His first order was to lower all boats to the rail. This order was obeyed as far as it possibly could be. He then called out, "Women and children first." The order was then given to hard-a-starboard the helm with a view to heading towards the land, and orders were telegraphed to the engine-room. The orders given to the engine-room are difficult to follow and there is obvious confusion about them. It is not, however, important to consider them, for the engines were put out of commission almost at once by the inrush of water and ceased working, and the lights in the engine-room were blown out.

Leith, the Marconi operator, immediately

sent out an S. O. S. signal, and, later on, another message, "Come at once, big list, 10 miles south Head Old Kinsale." These messages were repeated continuously and were acknowledged. At first, the messages were sent out by the power supplied from the ship's dynamo; but in three or four minutes this power gave out, and the messages were sent out by means of the emergency apparatus in the wireless cabin.

All the collapsible boats were loosened from their lashings and freed so that they could float when the ship sank.

The Launching of the Life-Boats

Complaints were made by some of the witnesses about the manner in which the boats were launched and about their leaky condition when in the water. I do not question the good faith of these witnesses, but I think their complaints were ill-founded.

Three difficulties presented themselves in connection with the launching of the boats. First, the time was very short: only twenty minutes elapsed between the first alarm and the sinking of the ship. Secondly, the ship was under way the whole time: the engines were put out of commission almost at once, so that the way could not be taken off. Thirdly, the ship instantly took a great list to starboard, which made it impossible to launch the port side boats properly and rendered it very difficult for the passengers to get into the starboard boats. The port side boats were thrown inboard and the starboard boats inconveniently far outboard.

In addition to these difficulties there were the well-meant but probably disastrous attempts of the frightened passengers to assist in the launching operations. Attempts were made by the passengers to push some of the boats on the port side off the ship and to get them to the water. Some of these boats caught on the rail, and capsized. One or two did, however, reach the water, but I am satisfied that they were seriously damaged in the operation. They were lowered a distance of 60 feet or more with people in them, and must have been fouling the side of the ship the whole time. In one case the stern post was wrenched away. The result was that these boats leaked when they reached the water. Captain Anderson was superintending the launching operations, and, in my opinion, did the best that could be done in the circumstances. Many boats were lowered on the starboard side, and there is no satisfactory evidence that any of them leaked.

There were doubtless some accidents in the handling of the ropes, but it is impossible to impute negligence or incompetence in connection with them.

The conclusion at which I arrive is that the boats were in good order at the moment of the explosion and that the launching was carried out as well as the short time, the moving ship and the serious list would allow.

Both the Captain and Mr. Jones, the First Officer, in their evidence state that everything was done that was possible to get the boats out and to save lives, and this I believe to be true.

THE NAVIGATION OF THE SHIP

At the request of the Attorney-General part of the evidence in the Enquiry was taken in camera. This course was adopted in the public interest. The evidence in question dealt, firstly, with certain advice given by the Admiralty to navigators generally with reference to precautions to be taken for the purpose of avoiding submarine attacks; and secondly, with information furnished by the Admiralty to Captain Turner individually of submarine dangers likely to be encountered by him in the voyage of the "Lusitania." It would defeat the object which the Attorney-General had in view if I were to discuss these matters in detail in my report; and I do not propose to do so. But it was made abundantly plain to me that the Admiralty had devoted the most anxious care and thought to the questions arising out of the submarine peril, and that they had diligently collected all available information likely to affect the voyage of the "Lusitania" in this connection. I do not know who the officials were to whom these duties were entrusted, but they deserve the highest praise for the way in which they did their work.

Captain Turner was fully advised as to the means which in the view of the Admiralty were best calculated to avert the perils he was likely to encounter, and in considering the question whether he is to blame for the catastrophe in which his voyage ended I have to bear this circumstance in mind. It is certain that in some respects Captain Turner did not follow the advice given to him. It may be (though I seriously doubt it) that had he done so his ship would have reached Liverpool in safety. But the question remains, was his conduct the conduct of a negligent or of an incompetent man. On this question I have sought the guidance of my assessors, who have rendered me invaluable assistance, and the conclusion at which I have arrived is that blame ought not to be imputed to the Captain. The advice given to him, although meant for his most serious and careful consideration, was not intended to deprive him of the right to exercise his skilled judgment in the difficult questions that might arise from time to time in the navigation of his ship. His omission to follow the advice in all respects cannot fairly be attributed either to negligence or incompetence.

He exercised his judgment for the best. It was the judgment of a skilled and experienced man, and although others might have acted differently and perhaps more successfully, he ought not, in my opinion, to be blamed.

The whole blame for the cruel destruction of life in this catastrophe must rest solely with those who plotted and with those who committed the crime.

. . . .

The above is called the "Annex" to the "Finding of the Court." This latter I do not reprint for it consists only of 21 questions, the answers to which are found in the "Annex."

A notice in "The Daily Telegraph" (London) of May 12, announced that

"The Board of Trade have ordered a formal investigation into the circumstances attending the loss of the S.S. 'Lusitania,' and they desire to invite passengers of the 'Lusitania' who now are, or will shortly be in or near London, and who are able to supply evidence likely to be of value for the Inquiry, to communicate at once, either personally or by letter or telegram, to the Solicitor of the Board of Trade, at the Hotel Metropole, Northumberland Avenue, Charing-Cross, W. C.; with a view to statements being taken from them at the said address, between the hours of eleven A.M. and six P.M. during the week commencing Wednesday, the 12th instant, and ending, and including, Tuesday the 18th instant.

"The Inquiry will be conducted by the Law Officers, who may be relied upon to see that all material points consistent with the public interest will be dealt with."

I know that some passengers did appear and did make official statements which they signed. Others laid evidence informally before the Solicitor, and while they did not sign statements, they were in London during the Official Inquiry and could have been summoned and would have testified.

The following testimony, for example, was informally offered: that the portholes were open, that the discipline of the officers and crew was not what it should have been, that the collapsible boats were not fitted with oars and were not in proper working condition, etc. None of this evidence seems to have been desired by his Lordship and his Assessors, or at least there is nothing to show that it was ever laid before them.

I do not question the sincerity of the findings of Lord Mersey's Court, based on the evidence placed before it; but what became of this informal evidence, as quoted above, and much more that was laid before the Solicitor of the Board of Trade?

The Court finds that "*the portholes were closed.*" On what and on whose evidence? The above statement can hardly be made on the evidence of the Captain; for when he testified before the Coroner of Kinsale, in reply to the question, "What precautions did you take in connection with these threats?" (referring to the Notice from the German Imperial Embassy which appeared in the New York papers of May 1), he stated that "I had all the boats swung out and the bulkhead doors closed when we came within the danger zone." ("The Daily Telegraph," May 11.)

The Captain had the lifeboats swung out Thursday morning, twenty-four hours before the disaster, but I know of no evidence that shows that he ever ordered the portholes closed. If he had, it is fair to presume he would have mentioned it when he testified that he had ordered the bulkhead doors closed.

There is evidence that at least two lifeboats, each containing about fifty people, were dropped when almost 20 feet from the water. A survivor of one of these boats told me that the man for'ard, who had charge of the rope, simply let it run out through his hands. He was not one of the "frightened passengers" but one of the crew. It seems to me quite possible in this instance "to impute negligence" and "incompetence in connection with them" (the ropes).

In another part of the report Lord Mersey states that "no doubt there were mishaps in handling the ropes of the boats and in other such matters, but there was, in my opinion, no incompetence or neglect, and I am satisfied that the crew behaved well throughout, and worked with skill and judgment."

Just above this in the report one reads: "That, since the commencement of the war, the Cunard Company has lost all its Royal Reserve and Fleet Reserve men, and the managers have had to take on the best men they could get and to train them as well as might be in the time at their disposal." Is it likely that any officer could take untrained men and in a few weeks, or even months, make such efficient seamen of them that they could, in a disaster of this magnitude, work "with skill and judgment"? I do not believe it could be done.

As one of the passengers who was moving around the deck and saw the heroic efforts made by his fellow passengers to achieve that which the crew utterly failed to accomplish, I resent, with every spark of manhood that is in me, the finding of Lord Mersey's Court when he says that "Probably (the) disastrous attempts of the frightened passengers to assist in the launching operations" added to the "difficulties" the officers and crew found in trying to lower the boats.

I would suggest adding to the "difficulties" mentioned above the following: lack of discipline among the crew and the lack of expert knowledge as to the handling of the boats, knowledge that can come only to the well-trained crew.

He says of this wonderful crew that "many more than half of them lost their lives." I suppose that is because the other half "worked with skill and judgment."

It would seem that Lord Mersey measures "skill and judgment" by the number that were lost; and if so, why doesn't he pass the same relative judgment on the passengers who lost their lives? He mentions figures, but here are the totals: There were 1,257 passengers and 472 were saved. To have been consistent, he should have written after the paragraph, "In addition to these difficulties there were the well-meant but probably disastrous attempts of the frightened passengers to assist in the launching operations," the following: "Many more than half their number lost their lives." From what, pray? Because they were "frightened," or because the crew acted with "skill and judgment"?

It doesn't seem to me that this Court of Inquiry has stood up to its business like the historic Briton who isn't afraid to take his medicine, and place blame where it should be placed; rather, it has hidden behind the act itself, which it finds "was done not merely with the intention of sinking the ship, but also with the intention of destroying the lives of the people aboard."

So for the Captain, the Court finds that he acted with "the judgment of a skilled and experienced man, and . . . ought not . . .

to be blamed"; for the Crew and Officers, that their "conduct . . . was satisfactory. They did their best . . . and their best was good"; for the Cunard Line, that the "reduction of the steamer's speed was of no significance and was proper in the circumstances." And what does this honorable Court find for the passengers who entrusted their lives to the judgment of the Captain and those under him? To wit, that "some of the passengers attempted to assist in launching the boats . . . and did more harm than good," and that "the frightened passengers (made) probably disastrous attempts to assist in the launching operations."

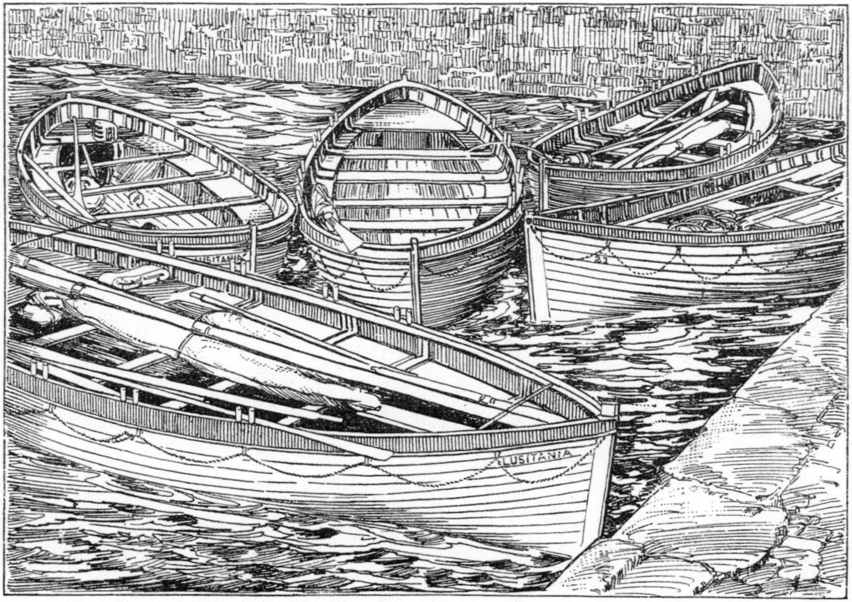

THE LUSITANIA'S LIFE BOATS IN THE SLIP AT QUEENSTOWN
(From a pen-and-ink drawing after a photograph)

The plans of the Lusitania here reproduced are from "Engineering" (London) in the issue for May 14th, 1915.

I think they are the plans originally published in that magazine when the boat was first put into commission in 1907. The arrangement and number of the lifeboats were changed a few years back and were different from those shown in the plan. On her last voyage there were eleven on each side, slung higher to allow space for the collapsible lifeboats that rested on the deck under the regular lifeboats. Also, this plan does not show the extra collapsible lifeboats that were nested out on the after deck. The launch that is indicated on the plan, I did not see.

THE CUNARD LINER "LUSITANIA;" LONGITUDINAL ELEVATION AND DECK PLANS.

CONSTRUCTED BY MESSRS. JOHN BROWN AND CO., LIMITED, SHIPBUILDERS AND ENGINEERS, CLYDEBANK.

Fig. 3

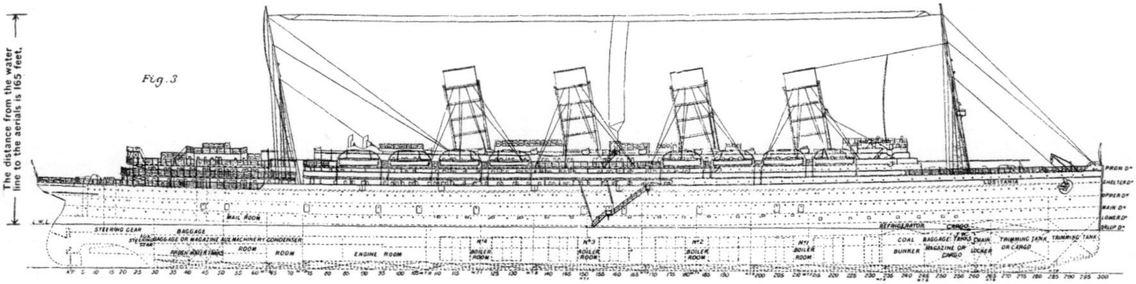

Fig. 4

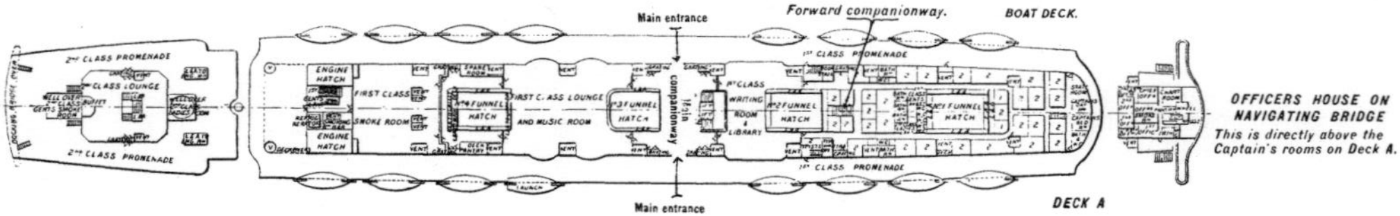

Fig. 5.

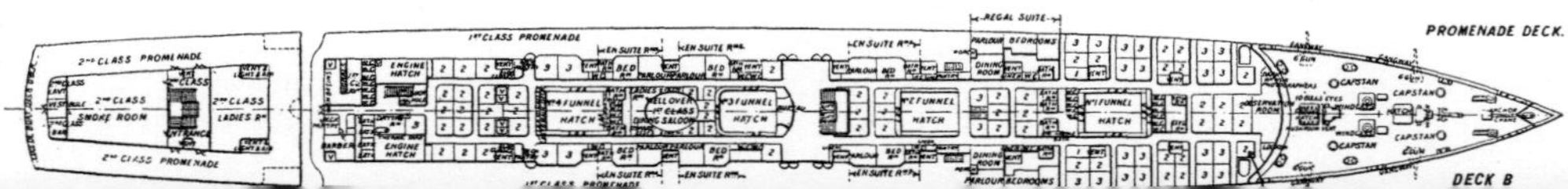

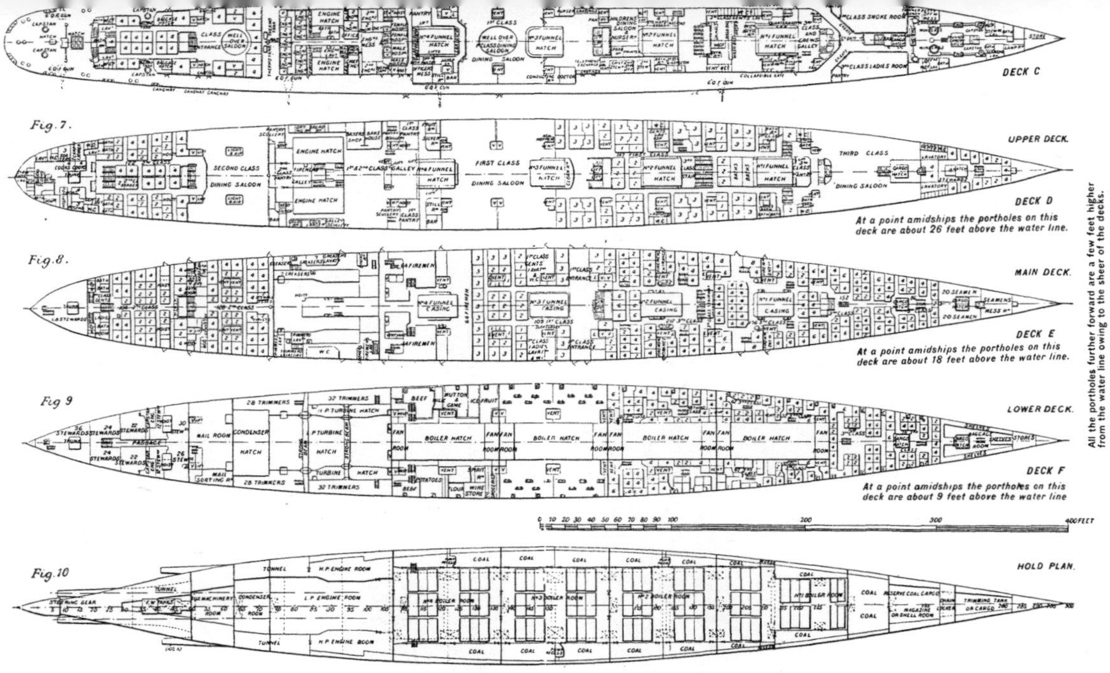
DECK C
UPPER DECK.
DECK D
At a point amidships the portholes on this deck are about 26 feet above the water line.
MAIN DECK.
DECK E
At a point amidships the portholes on this deck are about 18 feet above the water line.
LOWER DECK.
DECK F
At a point amidships the portholes on this deck are about 9 feet above the water line
0 10 20 30 40 50 60 70 80 90 100 200 300 400 FEET
HOLD PLAN.
All the portholes further forward are a few feet higher from the water line owing to the sheer of the decks.

Fig. 7.

Fig. 8.

Fig 9

Fig. 10

"And though thou thinkest that thou knowest sure
Thy victory, yet thou canst not surely know.
For we are all, like swimmers in the sea,
Poised on the top of a huge wave of fate,
Which hangs uncertain to which side to fall.
And whether it will heave us up to land,
Or whether it will roll us out to sea,
Back out to sea, to the deep waves of death,
We know not, and no search will make us know;
Only the event will teach us in its hour."